OUT OF THE PIT

Joseph's Story and Yours

Also by Larry L. Lichtenwalter

Well-Driven Nails

Visit our website at *www.rhpa.org* for information on other Review and Herald products.

OUT OF THE PIT

Joseph's Story and Yours

LARRY L. LICHTENWALTER

REVIEW AND HERALD® PUBLISHING ASSOCIATION
HAGERSTOWN, MD 21740

The author assumes full responsibility for the accuracy of all facts
and quotations as cited in this book.

This book was
Edited by Gerald Wheeler
Copyedited by Jocelyn Fay and James Cavil
Designed by Willie Duke
Electronic makeup by Shirley M. Bolivar
Typeset: Bembo 12/14

PRINTED IN U.S.A.

04 03 02 01 00   5 4 3 2 1

R&H Cataloging Service
Lichtenwalter, Larry Lee, 1952-
    Out of the pit: conquering life's difficult challenges

    1. Joseph (Son of Jacob). I. Title.

            220.92

ISBN: 0-8280-1432-9

BECAUSE JOSEPH HAS ALWAYS

BEEN HER FAVORITE, I DEDICATE

THESE VIGNETTES FROM HIS LIFE

TO MY WIFE, KATHIE

Contents

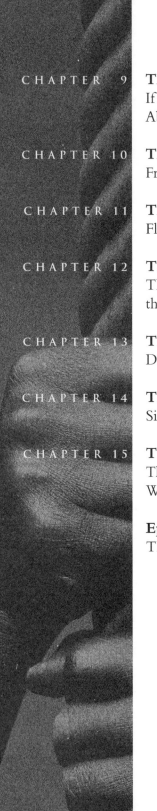

A Man for All Seasons

When our family visited England's infamous Tower of London, I was eager to tour the Bell Tower where the imprisoned Sir Thomas More spent his last days, and the Chapel of St. Peter in Chains, where they buried More's headless body. The British had a curious way of doing things in those days. They would behead their political prisoners out on Tower Hill, and then intern their headless bodies under the flagstone tile of the Chapel of St. Peter in Chains. The heads of those luckless victims would be stuck on a gibbet on the London Bridge for all to see and the birds to eat.

Some 1,500 headless bodies lie buried in the floor and under the altar of this infamous chapel. One gets an eerie feeling standing in that chapel that a thousand injustices and ghoulish deaths haunt the place. Suddenly Revelation's graphic imagery of "souls under the altar" crying out "How long, O Lord, holy and true, wilt Thou refrain from judging and avenging our blood" finds poignant meaning (Rev. 6:10).

Sir Thomas More had been the highest judicial official in England from 1529 to 1532. Both his public career and private and family life had been impeccable. But More resigned his lofty position because he couldn't conscientiously support King Henry VIII's plan to divorce his queen, Catherine of Aragon, so he could marry Anne Boleyn. The king finally executed More because the man couldn't honestly swear the oath of supremacy that would make Henry VIII head of the English Church and free to manipulate divorce law. More couldn't fake it, even though in reality he was one of the King Henry's most loyal, most honest statesmen.

Sir Thomas More stands out in England's history as an incredible man of integrity and conscience. A man whose moral and spiritual life was consistent through all the seasons of life. Robert Bolt produced a movie on More's life that he titled *A Man for All Seasons*. It was a fitting characterization of a life of uncompromising moral excellence.

It's a fitting characterization for Joseph as well. When I think of the biblical patriarch, those same words come to mind: "A Man for All Seasons." Genesis reaches a peak in these climatic last chapters on him. It's riches-to-rags-to-riches tale complete with every human passion—love and hate, ambition and glory, jealousy and fury. Tears of joy and grief are shed. Garments are rent in anguish. It's a gripping saga of treachery and deception, betrayel and forgiveness."[1] Through it all we see Joseph's rise from the darkest pits to vice-regal power. Woven throughout this magnificent story is the the theme of moral excellence, unswerving obedience, and relentless faithfulness to the living God.

Joseph's faithfulness takes place throughout life's changing fortunes. The good and bad. The heartache and blessing. The temptation and triumph. The story begins and ends in regal dress--a coat of many colors and Egypt's finest linen. In between those garment bookends Joseph wears the clothes of a slave and the rags of a prisoner. He literally rises up out of one dark pit to another. We will visit some of those agonizing pits—the pit of rejection, the pit of sexual enchantment, the pit of discouragement, the pit of power, the pit of painful memories, the pit of lost dreams, the pit of ungrace, and more. In the process we will learn where we can find the resources to ascend ourselves from their dark depths and any other pits that we may stumble into. We will find strength to conquer life's difficult challenges.

Genesis presents Joseph as different! He *is* different from every other character in this book of firsts. In the preceding stories of Genesis, the focus has been on God's faithfulness. Abraham, Isaac, and Jacob repeatedly fell short of His expectations, though of course they continued to have faith in Him. But in the Joseph story, we do not see him fail in any area. The biblical record presents not a single instance of moral or spiritual compromise. On the contrary, Joseph always responds in total trust and total obedience to God's will.[2]

Genesis presents Joseph, then, as "anticipation of what might yet still be, if only God's people would, like Joseph, live in complete obedience and trust in God."[3] The book was written for a generation of God's people waiting to cross the Jordan into the Promised Land. The fundamental principle reflected in Genesis 1:1—in the beginning—and the prophetic vision of end-times in the rest of Scripture is that the "last things will be like the first things" (Isa. 65:17; Rev. 21:1). The "beginning" of Genesis 1:1 already anticipates the end.[4] The scriptural vision of the future finds its fundamental moral and spiritual themes expressed already in the stories of Genesis. These foreshadowings are eschatological.[5] Joseph is a model of both the ideal person and the ideal people, accomplishing what Adam failed to do. His life looked forward to the Messiah yet to come. He casts a vision of what God's final generation of people can experience and must be!

We need to put on Joseph's colorful tunic and dream of a people as faithful as he! And in the process. let us catch a glimpse of our living God, whose providence and guiding hand always work things for good for those who love Him and have been called according to His purpose (Gen. 50:20; Rom. 8:28).

[1] Naomi H. Rosenblatt and Joshua Horwitz, *Wrestling With Angels* (New York: Delacorte Press, 1995), p. 315.

[2] John H. Sailhamer, *The Pentateuch as Narrative* (Grand Rapids: Zondervan Pub. House, 1992), p. 211.

[3] *Ibid.,* p. 215.

[4] *Ibid.,* p. 83.

[5] Warren Austin Gage, *The Gospel of Genesis: Studies on Protology and Eschatology* (Winona Lake, Ind.: Carpenter Books, 1984), pp. 3-15.

CHAPTER 1

Are We All a Little Crazy?

GENESIS 37:1-11

Are We All a Little Crazy?" *Newsweek* asked on its cover for an article on funnyman Robin Williams. Williams posed as a doctor holding a stethoscope to his own forehead, listening intently to what may be going on inside. He had a far-off look in his eyes, complete with frazzled hair. The subject? New insights on genetics and brain science. Recent genetic and neuroscience discoveries appear to show how genes, together with life's experiences, affect behavior by acting on and shaping the brain. The research suggests that something real, something genetic, something physical underlies our idiosyncracies and eccentric behaviors as well as our temperament, our moral spiritual inclinations, and our choices. One article has the title "My Brain Made Me Do It."[1]

Not only are all of us a little bit crazy, but our brains incline us toward what we do and how we feel. Obviously, multiplying the categories of mental illness isn't just a game—it has effects in the real world. While no one really wants to be labeled "sick," at times it may be better than the alternatives—litigation, prison, loss of employment, embarrassment, and guilt.

There is some truth, for sure, to all this. We are all a little crazy. The Bible announces that each one of us has a fallen human nature (Rom. 3:23; 5:12-19; Jer. 17:9; 13:23; Prov. 14:12; Isa. 1:4-6). We're the product of genes and environment. The very fabric of our psyche has evil woven into it. And yet, I will hasten to say, the image of God still remains in us, and we have not lost our freedom of choice or the reality of moral accountability. As one *Newsweek* article concludes: "Some people will be courageous, some shy, some vandals. But people will still be responsible for what they do."[2]

Consider, now, these thoughts on the patriarch Joseph:

"These are the records of the generations of Jacob. Joseph, when seventeen years of age, was pasturing the flock with his brothers while he was still a youth, along with the sons of Bilhah and the sons of Zilpah, his father's wives. And Joseph brought back a bad report about them to their father" (Gen. 37:2).

"These are the records of the generations of Jacob." "Joseph brought back a bad report." Genesis presents Joseph as having Jacob's genes and being in an environment affected by his brothers' evil influence. The next verse tells of his father's favoritism and the one after that, his brothers' hatred and rejection because Joseph snitched on them.

One of the struggles we have with Bible characters such as Joseph is the idea that they have some kind of an advantage over us. Perhaps a walk with God or a natural bent toward spiritual things and being good that the rest of us don't have. And so we read their story with an existential distance. They represent an elusive, unrealistic ideal out of touch with life as we know it. That's why we need to begin our sketch of Joseph's life with the very first pit he found himself trapped in—the pit of being human. Before we can dream of a people as faithful as Joseph and of a God whose providence works things for good, we must see the human Joseph.

The generation-spanning sins of his family had definitely shaped Joseph. He lived in a dysfunctional home dominated by lying, deceit, immorality, violence, favoritism, and manipulation. Remember those stories? How Grandma Rebeckah put his dad up to stealing Uncle Esau's birthright? How Granddaddy Laban swapped sisters on Jacob's wedding night? Or Dinah's rape and Simeon and Levi's slaughter of an entire village? How about his brother Reuben sleeping with one of his father's wives? Or the family's rivalry and jealousy and idolatry? If any young man had an excuse for turning out bad, Joseph certainly did. He could have easily blamed his dad, his mom, his brothers, and even his sister for the rest of his life—for repressed anger, lingering bitterness, fear of rejection, and a tendency to be deceitful, manipulative, and immoral. After all, he had lived in that kind of environment for 17 years.[3]

Joseph had both inherited and environmental shaping toward evil. And according to *Patriarchs and Prophets,* he had a few cultivated tendencies as well, faults that needed correcting. He was becoming self-sufficient and exacting.[4] Like any 17-year-old, Joseph enjoyed his father's favoritism, but in the process he became vulnerable in the midst of some very predictable temptations. He became a pain-in-the-neck tattletale dreamer who made his brothers see red. Joseph was a normal kid. Although he may have been head and shoulders above his brothers spiritually, that did not keep him from making some bad judgments.

The young man started out, then, in the pit of being human. Exactly where every one of us is—living in a fallen home, in a fallen world, with fallen human nature and selfish tendencies that want the world to revolve around ourselves. That's why when we dream of a people as faithful as Joseph, we envision those who ascend by God's grace from the dark depths of inherited and cultivated tendencies to do evil. The vision is for a people today who come forth from their fallen dysfunctional heritage as unsullied and unpolluted as Joseph did. And in so doing, hold forth the promise that God can do the same work in the lives of others.

Behind Us, the Weaver

In his classic on the life of Joseph, F. B. Meyer includes a poem by C. Murray about God's gracious providence:

> "Behind our life the Weaver stands
>   And works His wondrous will;
> We leave it all in His wise hands,
>   And trust His perfect skill.
> Should mystery enshroud His plan,
>   And our short sight be dim,
> We will not try the whole to scan,
>   But leave each thread to Him."[5]

Genesis tells how through the power of God Joseph rose above the negative influences in his environment and the negative tendencies of his own heart. He could escape his background because behind him stood the Weaver, who loved him and led him through each experience in a way that would grow him and sustain him and empower him. From the pit of being human he rose to the mountain of being like God. He cultivated a heart for God, one that chose to do what was right with God's help. Joseph allowed God to transform him into His image. And the Weaver did His work!

The story of Joseph is an account of how "God specializes in changing us and conforming us into His image, no matter what our family background."[6] Regardless of our inherited tendencies and no matter how fallen our nature, the Weaver does His work if we trust Him with our lives. God can do it. You can't and I can't. But God can! Joseph was a living example of that incredible truth. "God understands our particular circumstances and He wants to help us rise above the negative influences in our lives."[7] He will empower us to do so as we choose Him and His ways. Our resource to ascend from the pit of being human is the living God of heaven.

When we put on Joseph's colorful tunic and dream of a people as faithful as he, we must start where he did, with our fallen human nature and all those areas of our lives in which we are crazy with sin. But then we must place against the picture of where we are a vision of what God is able to do in us and through us if we but yield ourselves to Him.

This has nothing to do with perfectionism, but everything to do with victorious living through the grace and power of the living God of heaven. Through divine help we become partakers of the divine nature and overcome the corruption that sinful desire has unleashed upon the world (2 Peter 1:4). What is impossible with humanity—what is impossible with you and me—is possible with God (Matt. 19:26; Luke 1:37; Phil. 4:13; Col. 1:10, 11). While our fallen humanity will ever be a part of us till Jesus comes, God's activity in our lives renews His image within us until our true humanity shines forth. He works in us to enable us both to will and to do what He desires (Phil. 2:13). God strengthens us with power through the intervention of His Spirit in the depths of our inner being (Eph. 3:16). We become a new creation—with new thoughts, new motives, new passions, new life habits. In them the love of Christ so compels us that we no longer live for ourselves but for Jesus Christ alone (2 Cor. 5:14-17).

It is no accident that the only person that Genesis speaks of as being filled with the Spirit of God is Joseph. And that statement comes out of the mouth of an Egyptian Pharaoh.[8] The Holy Spirit was in his life, empowering him, transforming him so much that a pagan king could declare, "Can we find a man like this, in whom is a divine spirit?" (Gen. 41:38).

Our human nature has a part to play in fulfilling God's plan—it is to choose to yield our heart. Then the Holy Spirit works in a mighty and wonderfully powerful way. "When God's people respond as Joseph responded, then their way and God's blessing will prosper."[9]

During a Bible study with an elderly man, I asked him if he would have the assurance of eternal life if he were to die that very night. We had reached that point in the series in which a relationship with Jesus and an understanding of the gospel was crucial to our continuing study. "I would like to know that," he responded quietly after what seemed a long silence, "But I don't know how." Then I asked the basic question: "How is a person saved?" He began giving me as long list of things that he needed to do to be saved. So I took him to Ephesians 2:8-10 and we read these incredible words:

"For by grace you have been saved through faith; and that not of yourselves, it is the gift of God; not as a result of works, that no one should boast. For we are His workmanship, created in Christ Jesus for good works, which God prepared beforehand, that we should walk in them."

Reciting it slowly and carefully, I tried to emphasis the right words—"grace," "faith," "gift," "not of works." Then I repeated, "How is a person saved?" He responded the same way as before, enumerating a long list of things he needed to rectify in his life. So a third time I presented the passage even more slowly. Emphasizing again the important words of "grace," "faith," "gift," and "not of works," I said, "How is a person saved?" Five times I read Ephesians 2:8-10 to him and five times I received the same answer. Each time he responded with what he felt *he* had to accomplish.

On the sixth try I decided to explore with him the nature of a gift. "Do you buy a gift?" I asked.

He shook his head.

"How do you get it?"

"Someone gives it to you."

"Do you deserve it or earn a gift in some way?"

"No!" Then it began to dawn on him what the verse was saying. And when he realized that salvation was a gift, he demanded, "How do you get that gift?"

Here was a good man who'd lived a long life without doing anything really bad by most standards. But he needed to understand his absolute need of a Saviour. That he was in the pit of human fallen condition like everyone else and that the only way out of that pit was through the grace of Jesus Christ. Only the blood of Jesus Christ, the substitutionary atoning work of Jesus on Calvary's cross, could ever save him.

It is only as we accept the realty of where we really are and how much we need a Saviour that we ever feel compelled to yield our lives to the hands of the Weaver and allow Him to lift us out of the experience of inherited, cultivated, and environmentally formed tendencies. Only that will get us to the place where we partake of the divine nature and overcome sin's corruption. In the coming chapters we will see Joseph rise like a shining star of moral and spiritual excellence, thus becoming a paradigm of God's grace for a final generation. As his impeccable record unfolds before us, we must ever remember that he was as human as we are and just as in need of the same Saviour who covers us with His cleansing blood and robe of righteousness. It was in the midst of that saving relationship with God that Joseph found the power to be what God envisions all of us to be.

Jacob's death-bed blessing reminds us where such power comes from:

"Joseph, you are a fruitful vine growing near a stream and climbing a wall. Enemies attacked with arrows, refusing to show mercy. But you stood your ground, swiftly shooting back *with the help of Jacob's God, the All-Powerful One*—his name is the Shepherd, Israel's mighty rock. *Your help came from the God your father worshiped, from God All-Powerful.* God will bless you with rain and streams from the earth; he will bless you with many descendants. My son, the blessings I give are better than the promise of ancient mountains or eternal hills. Joseph, I pray these blessings will come to you, *because you are the leader of your brothers"* (Gen. 49:22-26, CEV).

Here is the secret of ascending out of any pit—and for sure the pit of fallen human nature and its predicament of lostness. It is God alone—the All-Powerful One. Did you know that the blessing Jacob prayed upon Joseph can come to you? The same God who helped Joseph can also transform your life. You, too, can be a moral spiritual leader—no matter how crazy you are. You only need to confess your condition, your need, and cling to Him—the All-Powerful One.

---

[1] *Newsweek,* Jan. 26, 1998.

[2] *Ibid.*

[3] Gene A. Getz, *Joseph: Overcoming Obstacles Through Faithfulness* (Nashville: Broadman and Holman, 1996), p. 11.

[4] Ellen G. White, *Patriarchs and Prophets* (Mountain View, Calif.: Pacific Press Pub. Assn., 1958), p. 213.

[5] C. Murray, as quoted in F. B. Meyer, *The Life of Joseph* (Lynwood, Wash.: Emerald Books, 1995), p. 9.

[6] Getz, p. 11.

[7] *Ibid.*

[8] This does not mean that Pharaoh became a believer in the one true God. Rather he simply acknowledged that Joseph's wisdom and skill were more than natural human achievements. When we remember that before interpreting Pharaoh's troubling dream, Joseph emphatically instructed him that "it is not in me; God will give Pharaoh a favorable answer" (Gen. 41:16; see also verses 25, 28, 32), we should not be surprised at Pharaoh's observation. While Pharaoh didn't know anything about the Holy Spirit per se, he had just witnessed the Spirit's power in the life of one of God's servants. In an unwitting way, this pagan king enunciated both a truth and theme in Joseph's story. The thought of the Spirit of God as the enduring source of inward illumination and intellectual power finds expression elsewhere in the Pentateuch, such as Exodus 31:3 and Numbers 27:18. See also Daniel 2:47 and 3:28, 29 in which a pagan king enunciates truths about God after both being instructed about Him and then seeing Him at work.

[9] J. H. Sailhamer, *The Pentateuch as Narrative,* p. 211.

CHAPTER 2

The Spitting Cell

GENESIS 37:2-5, 12-20, 23-28

Have you heard of the spitting cell? Albert Camus tells us about it in his novel *The Fall*. The spitting cell is a walled closet high enough for a prisoner to stand up in but with no room for him to move his arms. The solid door that locks him in his cement shell stops at chin level, leaving only his face visible. The shape of the closet prevents him from turning his head. Every passing jailer spits copiously in the prisoner's face. And they make it a point to come by often. The prisoner, wedged into his cell, cannot wipe his face. All he can do is close his eyes.[1] Trapped there, all he can do is feel shame and scorn.

In a few terrifying moments Joseph learned firsthand what a spitting cell was all about.

When Joseph's brothers saw him on the horizon, their eyes glazed with hostility. They could not possibly miss who was coming across the field in his magnificent coat. Even at a distance he looked like a prince rather than a fellow shepherd. The sight of that "richly ornamental robe" was like waving a red cape in front of a testy bull—in this case, 10 "bulls." "Here comes this dreamer!" they sneered (Gen. 37:19). "Come and let us kill him and throw him into one of the pits," they must have shouted among themselves. Their voices trembled with anger. "Then let us see what will become of his dreams" (verse 20).

Joseph continued to approach—innocent, unsuspecting of danger—and encountered glares, insults, and taunts. Within moments his brothers stripped him of his robe, rudely dragged him to an open pit, and threw him in. There they left him to die while they sat down to eat. In the end, they sold him as a common slave to a merchant caravan traveling south.

The pit of rejection—that's where we find Joseph. The rejection he felt must have been extremely intense, creating severe anxiety. Potential rejection and abandonment haunts every human relationship. Our friends can turn their backs on us, our children can spurn us. Parents may disown us or our spouse divorce us. A church may abandon us and leave us alone in the midst of our pain and need. Or our employers can tell us they no longer need us.

Rejection respects neither gender, social class, intelligence, education, race, or any other consideration. It's a tragic fact in many of our lives and causes constant fear. Or it may produce shame, guilt, depression, anger, hostility, or aggression.[2] Rejection begins early in life and can be at the heart of much of the moral dysfunction we exhibit in interpersonal relationships.

When we put on Joseph's colorful coat and dream of a people as faithful as he, our imagination will linger long on his experience in the pit of rejection. Joseph's story can carry us through our own pit of rejection, easing its impact on our moral and spiritual life as well.

Robes of Identity

In his book *Man's Search for Meaning* Nazi death camp survivor Viktor Frankl shares his experience of life in a concentration camp. He does not write of facts and events, but personal experiences of how everyday life in a concentration camp reflected itself in the mind and feelings of the average prisoner. Frankl tells of arriving in Auschwitz and being processed along with other prisoners. The guards asked him to strip, and he stood totally naked except for his wedding band. That, too, the guards removed. When he appealed for them to spare a manuscript of a scientific book that he had been working on—his life's work—they mockingly discarded it. Then they herded him to another room where they removed every hair on his body and shoved him toward the shower. "While we were waiting for the shower," he wrote, "our nakedness was brought home to us: we really had nothing now except our bare bodies—even minus hair; all we possessed, literally, was our naked existence."

"What else remained for us as a material link with our former lives?" he asked.[3] The camp had taken everything away and reduced Frankl to a nobody. He had become only a number tattooed on his arm and on the camp roster—and he felt it.

The experience of rejection ultimately has to do with our sense of identity and belonging—who I am, and where I belong. Sometimes tangible material things can symbolize our identity—a wedding band, a manuscript ready for publication, the hair on our body.

Joseph's symbol of identity was the richly ornamented robe his father had given him. It was a special gift. Some translators call it "a coat of many colors." However, it was far more than a typical garment with a few added touches of finery. The sleeves reached to the wrists and the main body of the coat dropped to the ankles. Beautifully tailored and decorated, it was the kind of coat worn by royalty. King David's daughter, Tamar, wore "a richly ornamented robe" (same Hebrew word), which, Scripture tells us, "was the kind of garment the virgin daughters of the king wore" (2 Sam. 13:18, NIV). When Tamar's brother Amnon raped her, she "put ashes on her head and tore the ornamented robe she was wearing. She put her hand on her head and went away, weeping aloud as she went" (verse 19, NIV).

I find this reference to Tamar's "richly ornamented robe" important in understanding the significance of Jacob's gift to Joseph. It represented the moral purity and moral excellence that was assumed among the princesses. Prior to Tamar's defilement by her brother, she was a virgin. Once he disgraced her, she immediately removed the robe and tore it to pieces. She no longer considered herself pure.[4]

Patriarchs and Prophets tells us that Joseph had a "widely different character" from his brothers.[5] Jacob's sons were not noted for their purity, gentleness, or truthfulness. In fact, the "bad report" Joseph had given to his father about his brothers probably involved some kind of immorality. Joseph's oldest brother, Reuben, had bedded Bilhah, one of his father's wives (Gen. 35:22). And another brother, Judah, impregnated his own daughter-in-law, thinking she was a cult prostitute (Gen. 38:1-26). Whatever their character or deed, though, "every time his brothers saw Joseph wearing this beautiful coat, they were reminded of the contrast between themselves and him."[6] He devoted himself to truthfulness and purity—and they did not.

Joseph's coat also symbolized position and status. It was not the kind of coat worn by a common shepherd. Rather it was the garment of a favored son who had a high position in the family. It is possible that because of his moral and spiritual character, Jacob intended to pass the birthright to Joseph.[7] At least, that's what his brothers feared. Only persons of distinction displayed such costly coats, and they knew it.

In short, Joseph's coat stood for his identity—his status, his moral purity. It depicted who he was, what he was like, and the position he held in the family. In our story Joseph's colorful robe becomes a symbol of acceptance, a flashpoint for jealousy, and a vehicle for debasement. It had been given in love, but ripped off in hatred.

Tearing the coat from him was a deliberately demeaning gesture, a dehumanizing experience. The Hebrew word employed here *(pashat)* is the same word used elsewhere in Scripture for cutting the skin off an animal sacrifice with a knife (Lev. 1:6; 2 Chron. 29:34; 35:11). Something both disfiguring and grisly, it represented a violent and radically dehumanizing or demeaning act (Job 19:9; 22:6; Eze. 16:39; Hosea 2:3). Micah refers to those "who eat the flesh of my people, strip off their skin from them, break their bones, and chop them up as for the pot and as meat in a kettle" (Micah 3:3). Joseph's brothers, then, literally ripped away the symbol of who Joseph was. They disfigured his psyche, violated his self-worth, and crushed his spirit. In effect the act said, "This is not what you really are. You are not important. In fact, you are no better than an animal to be skinned or thrown in a pit. A useless slave to be sold to pagans." Joseph's brothers were reacting to who he was—to his moral life and status. They repudiated his disruptive dreams with their threat to change status and position in the family. As Lewis Smedes writes, people shame us (reject us) because they feel shamed by us.[8] We threaten them.

Rejection is the loneliness of living abandoned and isolated from those who mean the most to us. It comes when our own people—those we most need to accept us—weigh and find us unacceptable.[9] An emotionally charged knowledge, rejection tells us that others do not love or want us or consider us important.[10] We need to believe that we are desired and important not for what we can do, or look like, or provide, but just for ourselves. But to be rejected makes us feel under suspicion—that we are an object of scorn instead of a person to love.[11] One needs to belong to a real community to feel the shame of being shut out of it. That is why a close family living in a tightly knit community is the most effective shamer of all.[12]

As rejection chips at our identity and sense of belonging it can drive us to surrender to peer pressure so we can fit in and belong somewhere else. Or it can force us into dysfunctional behavior so we can get attention. Some seek to excel in something so that they will become known and valued. Many accumulate things as part of their identity. Others become despondent, suicidal, aggressive. The fear of rejection breeds all kinds of moral compromises and tangible expressions of hurt. Too many of us bury our feelings in reaction to people who hurt us.

Young people in particular need acceptance more than the average person. To be rejected by their peers is the most devastating thing that can happen to them. That is why so many of them will engage in risky activities against their better judgment rather than face being ostracized by the group. Joseph was at an age when he too needed acceptance. It is important to notice, though, that he would not find it because he had committed himself to things that alienated his brothers and denied him their acceptance.[13]

A Camel's Ride

But how do we escape the pit of rejection? To put on Joseph's colorful coat and dream of a people as faithful as he was means coming to grips with our own experience of rejection. We must wrestle with our own identity and sense of belonging. How did Joseph make it? What was his source of strength? Where was his sense of being during his terrible time of rejection and abandonment and isolation in his life?

The very last verse of Genesis 37 gives a clue: "Meanwhile, the Midianites sold him in Egypt to Potiphar, Pharaoh's officer, the captain of the bodyguard" (verse 36). That little word "meanwhile" is significant. While his brothers dipped his colorful robe in sheep's blood and presented it to his father as evidence of his death, something was going on in Joseph's heart. *Patriarchs and Prophets* tells us that as the caravan journeyed southward toward the boarders of Canaan, Joseph could see in the distance the hills sheltering his father's tents. He wept bitterly at the thought that he would never see his father again. Then he began examining the day's events. Graphic images of the way his brothers had treated him began to race through his mind. Their angry faces loomed vividly before his eyes. He replayed it again and again in his mind. The stinging, insulting words that had met his agonizing pleas rang in his ears.

So it was with a trembling heart that Joseph looked to the future. He was alone and friendless. What would be his lot in the strange land to which he now journeyed? For a time Joseph surrendered to uncontrolled grief and terror. At this point it would have been easy for him to have done what many do when they experience such devastating rejection—abandon their lives to sensuality and moral compromise as cover for how they felt inside.

But then his thoughts turned to his father's God. Joseph remembered all the things he had learned about Him. He chose to believe that the God of his father would be his God. "He then and there gave himself fully to the Lord, and he prayed that the Keeper of Israel would be with him in the land of his exile. His soul thrilled with the high resolve to prove himself true to God—under all circumstances to act as became a subject of the King of heaven. He would serve the Lord with undivided heart; he would meet the trials of his lot with fortitude and perform every duty with fidelity. One day's experience had been the turning point in Joseph's life."[14]

Joseph "learned in a few hours that which years might not have taught him."[15] In that little meanwhile, there on the back of a camel, Joseph ascended from the pit of rejection to a relationship with God.

Although Joseph didn't handle it right at first, as the moments passed and he rode farther and farther from home, he finally found his identity and sense of belonging in God. He would not define himself by external things or other human beings. Throughout his story Joseph will change his clothes many more times as his circumstances alter—*but he will no longer feel rejection,* because he has firmly rooted his identity and sense of belonging in the living God of heaven. God loved him; he was important to God and belonged to Him. Now as God's son he would live for God.

When we put on Joseph's colorful coat and dream of a people as faithful as he, we imagine a people who ascend from the pit of rejection because they have come to know with confidence God's love for them. They have experienced His gracious unconditional acceptance and rooted their identity and sense of belonging deep in their relationship with Him. Each of them have come to know their Redeemer, Himself a person acquainted with grief and sorrow. Who Himself endured hostility from His own people and cried from Calvary's cross the most anguished words of rejection ever uttered by human lips—"My God, my God, why hast thou forsaken me?" (Matt. 27:46, KJV).

The thing that brings the deepest sense of rejection in our lives is sin and all the guilt and shame that our failures inevitably bring. When we've really blown it, we feel as if we're standing in the middle of a circle with a thousand fingers pointing at us and a thousand voices shouting, "Shame, shame, double shame, everybody knows your name." Some of us feel that kind of shame and rejection even after little failures. The exciting truth about the God of Joseph is that He does know your name, and you don't have to fear that fact. As Philip Yancey writes so masterfully in his *What's So Amazing About Grace?* "There is nothing we can do to make God love us more. . . . And . . . there is nothing we can do to make God love us less. . . . God already loves us as much as an infinite God can possibly love."[16]

Rejection exposes a longing for grace. Our world thirsts for grace in ways it does not even recognize. Grace comes free of charge to people who do not deserve it. Joseph didn't deserve it. Neither do we. Yet God loves us unconditionally. Completely. Always.

And so through a heartfelt trust in God's gracious presence, Joseph ascends from the pit of rejection to an intimate relationship with God. He becomes a pattern for you and me to do the same.

Perhaps you find yourself right now in the pit of rejection. You feel abandoned by your spouse, siblings, church, colleagues at work, or even God. If so, I invite you to hear the words of Psalm 27: "When my father and my mother forsake me, then the Lord will take me up" (verse 10, KJV).

Has some moral or spiritual decision in your life raised insurmountable barriers? Then hear the words of Jesus: "Blessed are you when men hate you, and when they exclude you, and revile you, and cast out your name as evil, for the Son of Man's sake!" (Luke 6:22, NKJV).

Hear the words of promise and assurance that tell us nothing can separate us from God's love. We can do nothing that will make God love us more. And nothing we do will make Him love us less. God loves us. Period! End of story.

And if by chance you happen to be a vehicle or an agent of rejection in someone else's life, may the grace of God so overwhelm you and flood your heart that you can only offer grace to that other person as well.

---

[1] Albert Camus, *The Fall* (New York: Vintage Books, 1956), pp. 110, 111.

[2] See John Joseph Evoy, *The Rejected: Psychological Consequences of Parental Rejection* (University Park, Pa.: Pennsylvania State University Press, 1983), p. 53.

[3] Viktor E. Frankl, *Man's Search for Meaning* (New York: Washington Square Press, 1984), pp. 21, 32-34.

[4] G. A. Getz, *Joseph,* pp. 21, 22.

[5] E. G. White, *Patriarchs and Prophets,* p. 209.

[6] Getz, p. 22.

[7] White, p. 209; Getz, p. 23.

[8] Lewis B. Smedes, *Shame and Grace* (San Francisco: Harper San Francisco, 1993), p. 56.

[9] *Ibid.,* p. 53.

[10] See Evoy, p. 14.

[11] *Ibid.,* p. 55.

[12] *Ibid.,* pp. 56, 57.

[13] Stuart Brisco, *Genesis* (Dallas: Word Publishing, 1987), p. 306.

[14] White, p. 214.

[15] *Ibid.,* p. 213.

[16] Philip Yancey, *What's So Amazing About Grace?* (Grand Rapids: Zondervan Pub. House, 1997), p. 70.

CHAPTER 3

Hitting the Top When You Reach Bottom

GENESIS 39:1-6

Have you seen Chris Fabry's *The 77 Habits of Highly Ineffective Christians?* It's a witty little book that tells how you can develop a weak and meaningless Christian life. Fabry identifies 77 habits that will snuff out the light of any on-fire Christian.

If your goal is to be an ineffective Christian, this book is a must! You'll learn such habits as guiding others with guilt, regarding worship as optional, holding grudges, forcing your spouse to meet all your needs, approaching church like a consumer, being negative, making prayer occasional, and more! There are even a few suggested songs you can sing along the way toward Christian ineffectiveness—"Just a Further Walk From Thee" and "Sweet Minute of Prayer."[1]

Fabry's Habit No. 59 he entitled "Embrace the Triangle of Mediocrity." He uses a simple sketch to illustrate his point. At the bottom right corner of a triangle he has written the words "Natural Abilities." The bottom left corner has the words "Spiritual Gifts." "Desire" perches at the top of the pyramid. In the middle of the triangle Fabry has drawn a comfortable-looking couch.

His point? If you want to be an ineffective Christian, be sure to sit on the couch of mediocrity and never ever allow your desire to galvanize your natural abilities and spiritual gifts toward anything meaningful in life.[2]

I'm sure it would have been easy for Joseph to have sat on the couch of mediocrity when he reached Egypt. After all, he was just a common slave in a land where they spoke a language he couldn't understand. Just one of thousands in a vast human market that filled Egypt's demand for slave labor. There simple survival meant avoiding the frown or the lash of your taskmasters. Slavery meant you were someone else's property. You did what they told you—period.

Scripture does not tell us anything about Joseph's first duties in Egypt. We can assume, however, that he performed the most menial tasks under constant supervision and surveillance. Joseph had reached the bottom of the human status ladder. Life had thrust him into the pit of the ordinary.

But his character and faithfulness in little things eventually became obvious to Potiphar. Whatever Joseph did, insignificant as it may have been, he did well.[3] He conducted himself with a difference as he worked, obeyed, and listened. At some point Potiphar transferred Joseph to his house. Again the Asiatic slave's behavior and industry were outstanding and above reproach. Potiphar's confidence in Joseph increased to the point that he appointed Joseph as his personal assistant over absolutely everything in his life. A man of power and wealth, the captain of Pharaoh's bodyguard, the chief executioner of the land, he turned absolutely everything in his house and in his life over to a common slave. It meant supervising all the other servants and employees, handling Potiphar's public relations, overseeing his finances, and administering his agricultural interests and all of his other business activities.

Joseph's experience graphically and powerfully illustrates what Jesus meant when He said being "faithful with a few things" prepares us (enables us) to be put "in charge of many things" (Matt 25:21). Joseph used what he had at his disposal—did his best where he was—and God honored his efforts. When Joseph reached bottom, he really hit the top. He ascended from the pit of the ordinary to the heights of extraordinary excellence in little and seemingly inconsequential things. In the process, Joseph's life teaches us that no task in life is meaningless or insignificant. Nor is any station in life unimportant or immaterial. He demonstrates that no responsibility is too small or inconsequential. Why? Because integrity in the seemingly little things forms and reveals character. Most of all, it honors God!

Majoring in Minors

A. A. Proctor suggests just how important humble service in little things might be:

> "Many, if God should make them kings,
> Might not disgrace the throne He gave;
> How few who could as well fulfil
> The holier office of a slave!"[4]

The holier office of a slave? Can you really hit the top when you've reached the bottom? This chapter's title, by the way, is a twist on Steven Berglas's book *The Success Syndrome: Hitting Bottom When You Reach the Top*. In it he talks about the moral, interpersonal, and psychological perils of success in our modern society. Berglas traces some of the pain and moral compromise that come with such success. People hitting the top often reach bottom in their moral and spiritual life.[5] They may find their family shattered and left far behind, or they can get caught up in destructive addictions and behaviors to meet the emptiness in their hearts or alleviate the stress in their lives.

Most of us, though, find ourselves in the pit of the ordinary. And many of us unfortunately remain at the bottom when we reach there. We stay average when we see ourselves as average. Fabry's couch of mediocrity is so easy to rest on. The pit of the ordinary somehow lulls us asleep and robs us of a passion for excellence wherever we might happen to be in life. Somehow we forget that every station in life has moral and spiritual value to it no matter where we are, no matter what opportunities come our way, no matter our education or status in life.

The pit of the ordinary is those moments in life, those details, those responsibilities that appear insignificant, meaningless, unattractive, or banal. They may lack obvious moral significance or spiritual value. Their mere mundaneness makes it easy to become careless, cut corners, or be less than our best. Little things become unimportant in our thinking, and self-worth and self-esteem sink into discouragement. The common and humdrum appear so dull that we think they belong only to the *losers* of society. The pit of the ordinary is whatever contemporary culture projects as not providing pleasure or prestige or power, or not able to release your greatest potential. Our world seems to tell us that there's no honor in the ordinary!

But Joseph didn't look at the ordinary in that way. In his classic on the life of Joseph, F. B. Meyer writes: *"though stripped of his coat, Joseph had not been stripped of his character."*[6] In our previous chapter we learned that Joseph ascended from the pit of rejection through the assurance of a relationship with the living God. On his way down to Egypt on the back of a camel Joseph looked across the horizon and saw the tents of his father and said to himself, "I will claim my father's God and I will commit myself to my father's God." He determined "to prove himself true to God—under all circumstances to act as became a subject of the King of heaven."[7] Without doubt it included the decision that if he was going to be a slave, he would be the best of slaves. At that moment Joseph chose to be cooperative, not rebellious. He would be reliable, respectful, and faithful, and do everything to the best of his ability. Perhaps even more than asked. Joseph would do all this for God's honor!

Here's how Paul would put what was in Joseph's mind on his way down to Egypt— what was at the heart of Joseph's commitment to excellence in little things. To understand what Paul is saying, though, we first must remember that the Roman Empire during the first century had a vast slave population. The gospel offered men and women fettered by physical chains a freedom that no one could ever restrain. And yet the apostle told them to stay where they were.

"Slaves, in all things obey those who are your masters on earth, not with external service, as those who merely please men, but with sincerity of heart, fearing the Lord. Whatever you do, do your work heartily, as for the Lord rather than for men; knowing that from the Lord you will receive the reward of the inheritance. It is the Lord Christ whom you serve" (Col. 3:22-24).

That's what Joseph came to understand on his way down to Egypt. That in the end he would be serving Someone greater than any human taskmaster. In the course of time Joseph read God's will in the daily round and the common task. God had placed him in the pit of the ordinary at this point in his life. Later in life Joseph looked back on his days in Egypt and said, "God sent me" (Gen. 45:5). Joseph saw himself more as God's servant than Potiphar's.

The pit of the ordinary is not as insignificant as we might think. As William M. Taylor writes, "It is a thing of character."[8] The ordinary forms and reveals our character. I believe it spills over into moral spiritual issues of our life as well—those so-called gray areas or so-called little things that Scripture and Ellen White speak to us about. When we are sloppy in our work ethic or in those seemingly mundane little things of life, we are likely to be sloppy in those supposedly smaller moral and spiritual things of life as well. Are we minimalists, or are we desirous of doing, as Oswald Chambers suggests, our "utmost for His highest"?

When I was 16 my dad helped me get a job at Del's Gulf Station on one of the main drags of Reading, Pennsylvania. I remember getting out of school and walking each day the half hour or so through the streets of Reading to this service station, where I would pump gas, change oil, fix tires, and do minor mechanical repairs. When Del hired me, he said, "Larry, I'm going to give you a dollar an hour, and that's it. Don't come and ask me for more." That was OK for me. It was my first job away from home, and I was happy just to have the opportunity. So I worked for the first month for Del. I did all the tasks he asked me to do, learned all the things I needed to know. I ran that station alone from 5:00 p.m till closing time at 9:00 p.m. About the second month I realized I had a lot of free time on my hands. When people didn't need gas or repairs and I had finished all the routine chores Del had asked me to do, I would just sit there at the desk inside the office waiting. So, bored, I wandered into the back room and into the work bays. Lots of old tools, trash, and dust had accumulated here and there through the years. So I just started cleaning up some of the stuff. During the next couple weeks the gas station began to change noticeably in appearance. After another month or so you could tell a big difference. One day my boss came to me and said, "Larry, I've never had anyone work for me this way before. Especially a young person. I'm going to give you a raise." All I did was more than what I had been asked. And I did it well. Del couldn't miss it.

Genesis tells us that "his master saw . . ." (Gen. 39:3). In some way Joseph's achievements were measurable in material and worldly terms. His ethic revealed itself in tangible, concrete witness. Potiphar was not slow to note that as soon as he put Joseph in charge, everything in his house and his business took off. When people see things clicking together, they sit up and look. Potiphar observed things happening in his home and business. And he said, "Wow! Something's going on here." His attention focused on Joseph. Joseph's abilities so impressed Potiphar that he increasingly promoted Joseph to a higher and higher level until the day came when he handed over to him the complete running of his household and walked away. The Egyptian official recognized in his slave an incredible discovery.

It is important to note that Potiphar interpreted this in spiritual terms. He sensed and came to acknowledge that the secret of Joseph's achievement was his relationship to the Lord. Joseph's work ethic and personal life brought spiritual conviction to Potiphar. Something goes out from us for others to evaluate and feel drawn toward. Genesis 39 tells us that "the Lord blessed the Egyptian's house on account of Joseph" (verse 5). What Joseph did blessed Potiphar. Ellen White adds:

"God was glorified by the faithfulness of His servant. It was His purpose that in purity and uprightness the believer in God should appear in a marked contrast to the worshipers of idols—that thus the light of heavenly grace might shine forth amid the darkness of heathenism."[9]

The pit of the ordinary tries to convince us that little things are inconsequential. But God's Word affirms our need to major in minors. Little things form and reveal our character, but in the end they impart character as well. They influence other people. If a spiritual passion motivates our integrity in little things, then our influence will be spiritual as well. As Bruce Barton writes: "Sometimes when I consider what tremendous consequences come from little things . . . I am tempted to think . . . there are no little things."[10]

Inside Out

The story of Joseph's ascent from the pit of the ordinary is not a success story. It is not an illustration that you can drop into a secular setting and say, "If you do this you will be successful." Rather, it is a story of human faithfulness in little things and divine blessings because of that faithfulness in little things.

Five times the story tells us that despite the precarious situation Joseph found himself in—rejected by family and a slave in a foreign land—he was not ever really alone. The Lord remained with him.[11] "The Lord was with Joseph and he prospered" (verse 2, NIV). "The Lord gave him success in everything he did" (verse 3, NIV). God was with him and blessed him. The story is an account of divine blessing, not human success.

God calls us to faithfulness, to integrity in little things. In His eyes the little things are important for our own character, our witness, and our spiritual and moral values. Ezra Benson observed that "the Lord works from the inside out. The world works from the outside in. The world would take people out of the slums. Christ takes the slums out of people, and then they take themselves out of the slums. The world would mold men by changing their environment. Christ changes men, who then change their environment. The world would shape human behavior, but Christ can change human nature."[12]

Majoring in minors means doing the smallest things on the loftiest principles. "Whatever your hand finds to do, do it with all your might" (Eccl. 9:10, NIV). "He who is faithful in a very little thing is faithful also in much; and he who is unrighteous in a very little thing is unrighteous also in much" (Luke 16:10).

God summons us today to faithfulness in little things. In the pit of the ordinary, God calls us to excellence. That invitation to excellence has to do with faithfulness to Him. Then He is free to bless us and bless others through us. It will honor His name and give our life more meaning—it will never be ordinary.

---

[1] Chris Fabry, *The 77 Habits of Highly Ineffective Christians* (Downers Grove, Ill.: InterVarsity Press, 1997), p. 18.

[2] *Ibid.*, pp. 73, 74.

[3] G. A. Getz, *Joseph*, p. 54.

[4] As quoted in F. B. Meyer, *The Life of Joseph*, p. 23.

[5] Steven Berglas, *The Success Syndrome: Hitting Bottom When You Reach the Top* (New York: Plenum Press, 1986).

[6] Meyer, p. 24.

[7] E. G. White, *Patriarchs and Prophets*, p. 214.

[8] William M. Taylor, *Joseph the Prime Minister* (Belfast, Northern Ireland: Ambassador, 1997), p. 49.

[9] White, p. 217.

[10] Bruce Barton, as quoted in Stephen R. Covey, *The Seven Habits of Highly Effective People* (New York: Simon and Schuster, 1989), p. 287.

[11] Victor P. Hamilton, *The Book of Genesis* (Grand Rapids: William B. Eerdmans Pub. Co., 1995), p. 459.

[12] Ezra Taft Benson, as quoted in Covey, p. 309.

CHAPTER 4

Between the Devil and Me

GENESIS 39:6-12

Country pop star Alan Jackson sings a heart-wrenching song called "Between the Devil and Me." Its lyrics graphically portray a man lured by some powerful temptation that threatens to overwhelm and destroy him. Sometimes the lure of a forbidden object, person, or experience so attracts our attention, so absorbs our thinking, so promises us well-being and pleasure, that we find ourselves tempted to reach out and grasp it. It keeps calling and won't let us go. Each time it whispers, "It's all right. I'll be your friend." But something deep down inside—conscience—reminds us it's wrong. No matter what, it won't ever be right. Behind this enchanting snare lurks the devil. We know that it's the devil and that somewhere a fire burns and its flames threaten to engulf us. The confusing power of that masterful temptation is like rising smoke that blurs our moral vision and leaves us feeling overwhelmed and powerless. In the midst of the blurring smoke, though, we catch a vision of someone important to us. It's enough to keep us from falling. "Love is strong!" sings Jackson. That person may be all I see between the devil and me. But it's enough!

We can only imagine Joseph's experience with his master's wife. Given Potiphar's position and rank, she no doubt was an Egyptian beauty, deliciously dressed in some of the finest, most sensuous clothing of the land. It's been said that Egyptian linen dresses were so sheer that you could draw them through a finger ring. While people wore less clothing in such a hot climate and people paid little attention to that fact, she knew how to get through such cultural blindness. She knew how to get him to notice her. Day after day she openly flirted with him, brazenly suggesting they make love.

Joseph now finds himself in the pit of moral compromise. It would have been easy for him to see only this woman in all her tantalizing beauty. He was in the prime of his sexuality, handsome and well-built. Far away from any family restraint, it would have been so easy. Sexual relations in Egypt were casual, and both men and women had more freedom than in surrounding cultures. But Joseph refused and then avoided her. When she turned up the heat and things got really sticky, when the fire began to spread and smoke threatened to blur his moral vision, he ran.

Where does such character come from? In an age of moral compromise, what is the secret of Joseph's success against such powerful temptation? How did he come through it pure and without moral compromise?

More Is Seen

Jackson sings, "She's all I see between the devil and me." The reason behind so much moral compromise in our lives is perspective. Where our vision finds its focus. In the midst of temptation, it's easy to overlook important other things. Joseph clearly saw Potiphar's wife. He could not miss this enchanting Egyptian and all she had to offer. But he perceived more than his master's wife, more than a shapely body and the sweet taste of sensual pleasure. Because more stood between Joseph and the devil than a tempter.

"Now Joseph was well-built and handsome, and after a while his master's wife took notice of Joseph and said, 'Come to bed with me!' But he refused. 'With me in charge,' he told her, 'my master does not concern himself with anything in the house; everything he owns he has entrusted to my care. No one is greater in this house than I am. My master has withheld nothing from me except you, because you are his wife. How then could I do such a wicked thing and sin against God?'" (Gen. 39:6-9, NIV).

Potiphar and God—that's who Joseph sees amid the rising and blurring smoke. That's whom he perceives between himself and the devil who calls himself friend. It is significant that Joseph makes his case not on the basis of some moral standard, but on his accountability to the master who had given him everything except his own wife, and on his even greater accountability to God.[1] Potiphar and God. Not rules. Not standards. But accountable relationships. That's where Joseph focused his vision.

Where do we obtain moral muscle for the struggle against the powers of darkness? How do we withstand almost overwhelming temptation to compromise moral boundaries? Joseph found strength in two valued relationships. He could not bring himself to violate his trusted relationship with his boss nor, more important, his fundamental relationship with God.[2] His experience shows how the issue of personal relationships is strategically central to moral excellence. We will rarely deny ourselves for a mere list of rules and even less for an institution. But we will forego something in order to preserve a valued relationship, to keep from hurting someone we love or letting down someone important to us. Joseph M. Stowell observes that "a set of rules is rarely worth denying our passions their pleasure; valued relationships are always worth self-denial."[3] In Scripture, however, rules, principles, and values always protect and nurture healthy relationships between human beings and between human beings and God. That's why they are so important, becoming unnegotiable boundaries. Joseph here intuits the rules and standards of principled behavior within valued, accountable relationships.

While my wife, Kathie, was cutting hair in the kitchen one evening, one of our sons stated that he was writing a paper on a controversial issue as an assignment for one of his classes. He noted how most of his class had chosen such topics as abortion, ordination of women to ministry, and theater attendance. But he was going to write on President Clinton's affair with Monica Lewinsky and whether or not he should lose his job.

"I think he should!" exclaimed one of his brothers.

"Yeah!" he replied. "If it was anyone else, they would lose their job! If Daddy did something like that, he'd lose his job right away."

Kathie listened as two of our sons shared their conviction of what their father would never do. It filled me with awe when she told me about it later that night. I couldn't help wondering, *What else do they think that Daddy would never do? How would they feel if I did it? What would happen to their faith? How would their own moral vision change if I let them down?*

One of the forgotten factors in any moral compromise is our accountability to significant others in our lives. Such people trust us not to yield to temptation or cross moral boundaries. They include our children, our spouses, our fellow Christians. Last but not least, many of our non-Christian friends and associates look up to us. Having firm convictions and a desire not to violate their trust and bring them pain is a great source of moral and spiritual strength.

And so with God! Joseph did not want to hurt his God's reputation. We have to remember that Potiphar was watching everything Joseph did. And he was beginning to conclude that all the success taking place in his home had some kind of a link to Joseph's faith in his God. "For Joseph to violate Potiphar's trust in him would undermine any trust his master was developing in the God who made Joseph trustworthy."[4]

But moral compromise would also be a "sin against God" (verse 9, NIV), as Joseph put it. In some way, for Joseph to give in and compromise on the moral issue would not only affect God's reputation but somehow touch God's own person.

Joseph sees more than just Potiphar's enchanting wife—he recognizes Potiphar and God standing there. Because he sees more—because he perceives two valued relationships that mean so much to him—it strengthens him to resist and then run. In so doing, he rises from the pit of moral compromise.

A life, then, that isolates itself or mentally detaches itself from meaningful relationships puts itself morally at risk. And a life that has not cultivated a personal relationship with God is particularly vulnerable. Having few meaningful relationships leaves us with little reason to deny ourselves anything.[5] Refusing to be accountable to others opens the way to moral failure. If all we ever see between the devil and ourselves is that forbidden object, that forbidden experience, that forbidden person that attracts our attention and promises us well-being—if that's all, we'll always lose. But if we perceive the faces of those to whom we are accountable, the faces of those we love—most of all, if we see the face of God—we will find strength. The forbidden object, experience, or person will lose its enchanting power over us.

Grace Escape

Since God structures the pattern for moral restraint in the form of strategic and meaningful relationships, then the most important thing we can do is to build more of them. We must hold ourselves accountable to others and to God. And we must continually contextualize ourselves. That is, I'm a father. A husband. A wife. A Christian woman. A follower of Jesus Christ. A Seventh-day Adventist Christian with a mission in the world. I am an honest man. An employee in this business.

Two drunks stumbled out into a snowy night. Staggering down the street, they nearly stumbled over an old Eskimo woman freezing in the snow. She lay there in a stupor as soft white flakes of snow slowly covered the vomit she had spewed on herself. The two men debated what to do about her.

"Is she a drunk or a bum?" one asked.

"Ah, she's just a bum. She's been one all her life!" the other muttered.

"Yeah, she's just an old bum." And they turned to walk away.

Then one of them paused. "But who was she before that?"

"Ah, she was a whore in Alaska."

"Ah, yeah, she's just an old whore." Again they started down the street.

Another pause. "But she hasn't been a whore all her life. Before that?"

"I dunno, just a little kid, I guess. Someone's little girl."

"Well, a little kid is something. It's not a bum and it's not a whore. It's something. Let's take her in."

We need to see the people around us differently than we do. As we do so, we will hold ourselves more morally accountable in our relationships with them as well. It will make us more careful how we treat them and what we do with them.

A friend of mine told me of a sticky situation that he found himself in while traveling in Europe some time ago. He had booked a motel in an area of town that he wasn't really sure about. When he got there, he realized he was in a really seedy place. That night he stepped out for a bite to eat, and on his way back to his room he noticed three hookers following close behind. One of them picked up her pace and cozied up to him. As they walked along together, she said, "Come with me."

"Where?" he replied.

"Oh, over to my place," she said playfully.

"What for?" he asked with a straight face.

When she began getting more graphic about her proposition, he stopped.

"I can't do that!"

"Why not?" she asked with surprise.

"I'm married!"

"So what? No one will ever know! You don't have to tell."

My friend then took a piece of paper out of his pocket and said, "The Bible tells me that my body belongs to my wife. Here's her phone number. You call her. And if she says its all right, then you come tell me." And with that he turned away, leaving the dumbfounded woman alone.

"You're stupid," she cried out after him.

But he walked away with a free conscience. Why? Because he had reminded himself and those around him who he was, to whom he was accountable, and what he stood for. He contextualized himself, drawing moral boundaries for himself and others.

Contextualizing ourselves or others is a basic biblical principle. For example, Paul invites Timothy to relate to "older women as mothers, and the younger women as sisters, in all purity" (1 Tim. 5:1, 2). Purity must frame his total perspective.

Seeing people in the context of their family and friends, as a person, as one of God's children, as someone hurting, as someone with an open future if treated with dignity, or as in relation to oneself as a leader or friend or Christian holds incredible power in terms of marking moral boundaries. Like Joseph and my friend, we need to help others put us in context as much as we place them in one. We must always contextualize ourselves.

Our moral strength rises in proportion to how we nurture meaningful relationships. How close we allow ourselves to others and how close we permit others to approach us and to really know us. And accountability in relationships includes how close we allow ourselves to get near God as well. If God is only out there in the distance, it will be hard for us to follow His will and the moral principles He has given us. When we are far away from God, replicating His character and conduct will seem like too tough a chore. The forbidden object that beckons me will obscure Him. But when God is close at hand—in our field of vision and the central relationship in our life—then radical reformation and moral excellence become a priority. And the same thing will happen with other significant relationships in our lives.

Our passage ends with Potiphar's wife literally holding the bag—Joseph's clothes. Like his brothers years before, she's stripped him. She had grabbed his outer garment and pulled him close to her. And there with the scent of her perfume and her body she implored him to make love with her—"Come lie with me." But he pulled away from her, and as he did so the only way he could get free of her grasp had been to twist himself out of those clothes. As he ran from Potiphar's house, no doubt his vision filled with another painful moment of stripping—the vision of his brothers tearing off his clothes. It seemed like only yesterday that they had ripped off his prized multicolored coat that his father had given him. The vulnerability he now experienced was similar to what he had felt then.

As we have noted already, *"though stripped of his coat, Joseph had not been stripped of his character."*[6] Moral integrity is something that comes from within. She could tear off his clothes, but she could not remove his character. We are the only ones who can do that to ourselves. Only we can bring to ourselves the nakedness of moral compromise.

William M. Taylor urges that we "look well to the *character,* for that is the main thing, and the life that secures that for Christ is always worth living."[7]

First Corinthians promises that "no temptation has overtaken you but such as is common to man; and God is faithful, who will not allow you to be tempted beyond what you are able, but with the temptation will provide the way of escape also, that you may be able to endure it" (1 Cor. 10:13).

Do you believe that?

When Joseph reached for something deep enough and strong enough to fend off those sensual advances of Potiphar's wife, he found it in valued relationships. They are part of God's avenue of escape. The way to endure—through His grace and power—is to hold ourselves accountable and to look upon the face of those who love us and whom we say that we love. When we so focus our hearts and minds upon God and those we are responsible to, God will raise us, too, from the pit of moral compromise.

Some of us have not been so successful. We have compromised ourselves in some way. In so doing we have deeply wounded family members or people in the community or church. If that has happened, I want to remind you that Jesus forgives. And that He empowers us to build valued relationships anew. I want to remind us that when temptation becomes so confusing that we are in danger of being drawn away—when the fire burns and the rising smoke blurs our vision—the living God can and will use those significant relationships in our life to be strong for Him, for them, and for self.

---

[1] Eugene F. Roop, *Genesis* (Scottsdale, Pa.: Herald Press, 1987), p. 257.

[2] Joseph M. Stowell, *Following Christ: Experiencing Life the Way It Was Meant to Be* (Grand Rapids: Zondervan Pub. House, 1996), p. 86.

[3] *Ibid.*

[4] G. A. Getz, *Joseph,* p. 60.

[5] Stowell, p. 87.

[6] F. B. Meyer, *The Life of Joseph,* p. 24.

[7] W. M. Taylor, *Joseph the Prime Minister,* p. 64.

CHAPTER 5

Moral Cues From Young Lovers and the Oval Office

GENESIS 39:6-12

In view of what's happening to the values in our own society, Joseph's experience with Potiphar's wife is probably one of the most relevant to our lives today. We live in a culture in which sexual immorality prevails. Such a culture of immorality reaches beyond the immoral acts of individual people to constitute the very fabric of our society and the values it extols and promotes. Cameron's *Titanic* and Clinton's sex scandals have provided powerful examples of just where our world is today. During the first months of 1998 Hollywood and the Oval Office ran neck and neck in molding the American imagination on sexual ethics. One presented sexuality in a grand and gripping emotional drama; the other in tawdry gossip.

For 15 weeks running *Titanic* was number one in the box office. Winning 14 Academy Award nominations and drawing in more than $1 billion in revenues, *Titanic* was an engrossing 3¼-hour drama that combined a Romeo and Juliet forbidden romance, intense thrills, and a somber "it-really-happened" tragedy. But Cameron's version of *Titanic's* fateful maiden voyage is a perilous moral journey as well. It includes drunken carousing, profanity, nude modeling, and steamy love in a cargo hold. Just leafing through Cameron's *Titanic* at a bookstore—a large full-color coffee-table book complete with pictures from the production set, bits of history, the how-to's of special effects, and the psyche weaving it all together—reveals the subtle mix of moral themes pervading the movie. The drama rejects the class struggle, greed, and arrogance of the industrial age. But it champions young love.

Titanic projects the subtle image that teen sex is the stuff of adolescent dreams and lifelong memories. After all, the 101-year-old woman looks back at five days on the ocean as the most liberating and memorable moment of her life. That's why so many young people have gone back to watch it six or eight times. The average person does not leave *Titanic* with the feeling that teen sex or premarital sex is wrong. They find themselves caught up in the power of romance. And they ache because class snobbery forbade such romance between the poor and the rich. Finally, they grieve because the liberating passionate love that *Titanic's* heroes enjoyed for a few fleeting days ended in horrific tragedy and death.

Titanic is an emotional heartbreaker that subtly numbs the moral sensibilities on the question of sexuality. One Christian reviewer said: "Much has been said of *Titanic's* titanic budget. At more than $200 million, it ranks as the most expensive movie ever made. However, the highest price may be paid by teen moviegoers inspired to take their moral cues from the film's young lovers. What could have been a tender romance and a captivating history lesson is sunk by nudity, teen sex, profanity, and harrowing depictions of death."[1]

The moral cues coming from the Oval Office during those same months were just as blatantly permissive. Once the Monica Lewinsky scandal hit headline news that January, it saturated our nation with an open discussion about sexual matters. Our children learned all too much and all too fast as charges of sex and lies beamed into every home. The troubling thing was that most of the media, and, according to the polls, most Americans, seemed to focus on what was either legal or illegal about Clinton's actions rather than on the fact that if he did *any* of the alleged things, it would be morally wrong (not just illegal), and he would be a poor moral role model.

Surprisingly, the president's approval rating surged to an all-time high. As long as the economy was good and people had work and food on their table, who cared what the president did in private? It was his business. The public had elected him for what was above his belt. After all, he was only human and had a lot of stress on the job. So what was wrong with a little fun? It didn't affect national security.

The president's hair-splitting on the allegations seemed only to muddy the moral issues even further. When is sex not sex? Or an affair not an affair? Why would Clinton be willing to admit making love to someone who was not his wife, and yet not want anyone to call it adultery or an affair? The sad thing about it all was what was not being said about moral leadership and the abuse of power. Why was no one clearly articulating what was morally right in terms of sexual expression or what personal or national sexual values should guide us?

It was the same kind of moral climate Joseph found himself in. Sexuality permeated the Egyptian culture. Everyone was doing it! Sexual enchantments presented themselves on every side, especially in the royal court and among the elite. Masters had full use of their slaves. Slaves often had little else in life to enjoy. We can only imagine Joseph's experience with Potiphar's wife. Day after day she openly flirted, brazenly suggesting they make love.

Titanic Morals

Genesis tells us, though, that day after day Joseph refused to go to bed with her. He refused even to be with her in any way (Gen. 39:10). Joseph did everything he could to avoid both her and possible compromising situations. In the end, she set him up and he had to make an instantaneous decision based on a habit of moral orientation (verses 11, 12).

In the pit of sexual enchantment Joseph maintained his sexual purity. His story of faithfulness is a call for purity in a culture of immorality. Joseph's experience testifies that a man or a woman can resist the sexual enchantments of an impure and decadent world. It encourages men and women, young and old, that they can overcome temptation and be faithful to God. Jesus' followers can go against the tide of contemporary culture and stand out morally distinct.

Ellen White warns that sexual enchantments will be one of Satan's special temptations for a final generation. "As we approach the close of time, as the people of God stand upon the borders of the heavenly Canaan, Satan will, as of old, redouble his efforts to prevent them from entering the goodly land. He lays his snares for every soul. . . . He employs the same agents now as he employed three thousand years ago. By worldly friendships, by the charms of beauty, by pleasure seeking, mirth, feasting, or the wine cup, he tempts to the violation of the seventh commandment."[3]

If that is true, and in light of what we can see taking place in our own society in just Hollywood and the Oval Office, we need a clear look at Joseph's experience.

Former associate *Newsweek* editor Diane Hemphill McDonald stated the issue clearly. In an article entitled "Mom, What's Monicagate?" McDonald suggested that today's parents are giving up far too easily on teaching their kids about right and wrong. She asks a significant question: "If children see their parents lacking courage and conviction—and observe immaturity, irresponsibility and crumbling integrity in 'role models' at society's highest levels—what value system and behavioral guidelines can we expect them to adopt?"[4]

Hers is a plea for clear convictions and unequivocal moral boundaries. Parents need to stand up and take a position on such matters, because society is just not going to do it. We can extend McDonald's plea to include the church in both its nurturing and prophetic vocation. God's end-time people need firm moral and ethical convictions based on His value system.

That's where we find Joseph. He could resist the temptation to sexual compromise because he had firm moral and ethical convictions based on a divine value system. Not fuzzy on what was right and wrong, he was clear, convicted, and confident. "How then could I do this great evil, and sin against God?" he asked (verse 9). It was a "great evil," a "sin against God."

Where did Joseph get such conviction, such clear thinking on sexuality? I believe it important to remember that the story took place hundreds of years before God spoke the Ten Commandments at Mount Sinai. As far as we know, Joseph didn't have its principles in writing anywhere. And he certainly didn't get his conviction from his brothers or from the prevailing values of his contemporary culture. From our enlightened New Testament standpoint we would think that Joseph's knowledge of God's laws and sexual matters should be somewhat limited.[5] Nevertheless, Joseph was clearly convinced that sexual activity with another man's wife was not only "great wickedness" but also a "sin against God." End of debate!

"But that's adultery, not premarital sex," we might be tempted to say. Even our own sex-saturated contemporary society senses something wrong with adultery.[6] Certainly it was at least an unwritten value of his day as well. So Joseph's moral stand should be no big deal for many.

I can't help wondering, though. What if it had been an unmarried woman who propositioned Joseph? Say, Potiphar's daughter or an unmarried female servant who worked with Joseph in the house? Would that have been permissible? Would he have allowed himself that luxury?

Given the sexuality permeating Egyptian culture, I believe Joseph's response to Potiphar's wife says as much about sexual immorality as a whole as it does about adultery in particular. In other words, had Joseph been sexually active, or considered premarital sex OK, the woman's sexy appearance and erotic gestures would have bowled him over. When everybody's doing it, and the boss's beautiful wife comes on to you day after day after day—promising who knows what, and the opportunity to cooperate in a relatively safe secret setting—it's hard to keep your own natural desires and tendencies under control. Especially if her words "Lie with me" included the element of command as well as seduction. Then Joseph would be dealing with the reality of power as well as the danger of sexuality. It was a clear case of sexual harassment (though in the minority direction). "Joseph was well-built and handsome" (verse 6, NIV). She had the hots for him and went out of her way to raise his sexual temperature as well. Yet Joseph still resisted.

For someone who did not have Scripture in his hand as you and I have today, it is remarkable how Joseph's moral stance reflects biblical values. The Bible teaches that the only acceptable sexual contact between two people takes place in a committed and loving marriage relationship. It considers anything else evil and a sin against God. Scripture tells me that the issue of our sexual purity is not a matter of prudish rules or a list of do's and don'ts that have to be spelled out (although such clearly definable standards present needed moral boundaries for fallen human relations). Rather, it is a matter of *spiritual discernment*. And spiritual things, the apostle Paul wrote, are spiritually discerned (1 Cor. 2:9-15). Those who allow themselves to go down the path of sexual permissiveness unwittingly blunt their spiritual discernment and diminish their moral sensibilities. Those who maintain their sexual purity retain their moral sensibilities and are able more clearly to understand the spiritual issue revolving around sexual ethics. While the world may call it love, and we may have a wonderful feeling in our hearts, sexual expression is always wrong outside a committed and loving marriage relationship. If we compromise ourselves in any way from what God's clear Word says, we are following our own rules and lack the Spirit of God.

We must have firm moral and ethical convictions based on a biblical value system. And we need to hear the kind of things Paul taught new believers living a first-century culture of immorality: "God's plan is to make you holy, and that means a clean cut with sexual immorality. Every one of you should learn to control his body, keeping it pure and treating it with respect, and never allowing it to fall victim to lust, as do pagans with no knowledge of God. You cannot break this rule without cheating and exploiting your fellow-men. Indeed God will punish all who do offend in this matter, as we have plainly told you and warned you. The calling of God is not to impurity but to the most thorough purity, and anyone who makes light of the matter is not making light of a man's ruling but of God's command. It is not for nothing that the Spirit God gives us is called the *Holy* Spirit" (1 Thess. 4:3-8, Phillips).

Another translation phrases verse 8 this way: "Consequently, he who rejects this is not rejecting man but the God who gives His Holy Spirit to you" (verse 8, NASB). Sexual permissiveness leads ultimately to rejecting the Holy Spirit's voice to our soul. Spiritual discernment and sexual purity go together.

God's will for our lives is sexual purity. That's the only safe thing spiritually.

Some time ago I was trying to learn how to build a Web page. While I was browsing and downloading files from the Internet one night, a provocative advertisement kept appearing on my screen. I was connecting to information about creating Web pages, so the tantalizing blurb seemed out of place. But there it was, everywhere I turned. Just a three-inch-by-one-inch colorful poster of the partial face of a very seductive-looking woman. All you saw were her eyes, an inviting glance, and her hair lying softly across her cheek. "Click Me, I'm Free," it said. You could almost imagine her voice whispering from the screen. At first I avoided her altogether. But when she kept appearing at different websites that I visited, I stopped for a moment and looked at that combination of pixels—that's all it was, a combination of light and dark segments on the screen. Everything else existed in my mind. Anyway, I looked at that combination of pixels and said to myself, "No, you are not free. No matter what you say, no matter what you promise me, the moment I click you I have paid a price." It would have affected my own personal integrity. In some subtle way it would have eroded my relationship with my wife and how I view her as well as my relationship with God. And it would certainly have affected my integrity and spiritual influence as an Adventist pastor.

Joseph was able to resist temptation to sexual compromise because he consciously challenged his culture's prevailing value system. We see it in the way that he clearly stated his position to Potiphar's wife, flatly rejecting her proposition. Leaving no room for debate or discussion, "he refused," Scripture says. Furthermore, he removed himself from the situation. Joseph did all he could to avoid being caught in a compromising position.

Ellen White makes some interesting observations on Joseph's spiritual and moral hygiene. "Arriving in Egypt, Joseph was sold to Potiphar, captain of the king's guard, in whose service he remained for ten years. *He was here exposed to temptations of no ordinary character.* He was in the midst of idolatry. The worship of false gods was surrounded by all the pomp of royalty, supported by the wealth and culture of the most highly civilized nation then in existence. Yet Joseph preserved his simplicity and his fidelity to God. *The sights and sounds of vice were all about him, but he was as one who saw and heard not. His thoughts were not permitted to linger upon forbidden subjects.* The desire to gain the favor of the Egyptians could not cause him to conceal his principles. Had he attempted to do this, he would have been overcome by temptation; but he was not ashamed of the religion of his fathers, and he made no effort to hide the fact that he was a worshiper of Jehovah."[8]

According to *Patriarchs and Prophets,* Joseph guarded his thinking. In doing so, he purposefully engaged the prevailing culture around him. The things he was seeing, the values that were pressing upon him, he refused to study or respond to. He would not give himself the luxury of even thinking about them.

In those situations in which he had no control over his environment, he guarded his thinking against the verbal and visual stimuli by tuning them out. When he could control his environment, he purposefully removed himself from the stimuli. In both situations Joseph manifested spiritual discernment. Engaging his mind, he purposefully rejected and resisted the prevailing culture's value system on sexual matters and drew for himself moral boundaries based on God's value system.

We cannot afford to miss the lesson. Unless we are willing to own our identity as followers of Jesus and consciously challenge the values of our society, the moral flood of a culture of immorality will erode us away.

To engage a culture of immorality, we must label it for what it is. *Titanic* will say premarital sex is the desirable culmination, the natural consummation, of a sweet romantic love. It's so right. But Scripture says it is sin. The Oval Office will give the impression that sexual ethics is elusive, open to individual interpretation and taste. But Scripture calls us to a sexual ethic that indicates a high level of clear spiritual discernment. We must avoid as much as possible those things that heighten temptation and at the same time carefully guard the avenues of our soul (Phil. 4:8). If we have to, we literally need to run! That means taking a personal stand on any media events, movies, music, and relationships that would lead us toward moral compromise.

The February 1997 issue of *People Weekly* featured a full-page advertisement for the USA Network. At the top was a picture of a fellow softly but passionately kissing a girl on her neck. Her eyes were dreamily closed. An expression of exquisite pleasure radiated from her face. The rest of the page was the picture of a belly button. It advertised "Steamy Sunday Dramas." Now, get this! "Guaranteed to break at least 20 percent more commandments than any other Sunday night lineup."[9]

That's where our culture of immorality ultimately leads, where the media is taking us. Our fallen society seeks to draw us away from God, away from what is morally right. Perhaps you have been struggling with not being able to pray or with the fact that God's Word is boring to you. Worship doesn't seem meaningful, you lack spiritual power, and your sexual values have declined. Maybe—just maybe—it's because what the world serves up as entertainment has begun to sweep away your mind, heart, and emotions.

When I shared some of these thoughts during a Sabbath morning worship service, an elderly man came to me afterward saying, "Pastor Larry, I'm too old for this now. I'm glad I don't have to worry about these kinds of things anymore."

I looked at him for a moment, then put my hand on his shoulder as I said, "You know, brother, I want to tell you about my grandfather. My grandfather was every bit your age. When I would stay with my grandfather on his farm during the summers as a little boy he would talk and talk about sex. He created some graphic images in my young mind of the well-built redheaded teenage girl living just through the woods. He talked about what he'd do if he could get her alone. Thought I might have a better chance at it, though. With that kind of talk swimming in my mind, I had a hard time looking at her in any other light.

"So," I said to my elderly friend, "your body may not be able to do much anymore, but your mind still can." And ultimately that is what God holds us responsible for (Matt. 5:28).

It's not just men. I listened to an interview recently in which a 101-year-old woman shared her recipe for long life—lots of beer and lots of sex.

In Romans 16:19, 20, Paul writes, "I want you to be wise in what is good, and innocent in what is evil. And the God of peace will soon crush Satan under your feet." God's ability to crush Satan under our feet is proportionally linked to how innocent we are in things that are evil and how much our minds are filled with what is morally good.

Grace Escape

A large bronze statue of a nude woman called the *The Lorelei* perches on the Rhine River at St. Goarshausen, Germany. A shapely seductive woman, she sits on a rock in the flowing Rhine waters. You can't miss her. She has her elbow on her right knee and her gaze fixed down and slightly to her left. Her long flowing hair reaches down to the rock she's sitting on. It's her only covering. While in St. Goarshausen I picked up a postcard and the poem that

Heinrich Heine wrote about the legend that the nude statue represents. "The Lorelei" is about a bewitching tempter luring fishermen young and old with her song. When they see her while fishing on the Rhine, their hearts start to quiver and beat.

> "There's a man in his boat on the river,
> He cannot but listen and stare,
> A longing is making him shiver,
> Look out, the rock's ledge, oh beware!
>
> I fear there's a crash, the boat sinking,
> The man will be swallowed and gone,
> And that with melodious singing,
> The Lorelei will have done."[10]

That is exactly how a culture of immorality captivates people's minds, emotions, and psyche. The power and lure of the pit of sexual enchantment is incredible. It can so overwhelm us that we do not realize the danger we are in. Our culture of immorality is bewitching. Dietrich Bonhoeffer writes that when lust reaches fever pitch, "God is quite unreal to us" and Satan fills us with "forgetfulness of God." "When you have made your eye the instrument of impurity," he says, "you cannot see God with it." All we focus on is that forbidden experience or forbidden person.

But Joseph beheld the face of God. In a culture in which vice permeated everything around him with all kinds of sights and sounds, Joseph allowed his mind to dwell constantly on the face of God. It alone was his strength and protection, his way through the moral miasma of his day.

A culture of immorality reaches beyond individuals to the very fabric of society and the values it extols and promotes. But Joseph's experience is a call to purity. And if you have already compromised your sexual integrity, God graciously promises forgiveness and the wonderful miracle of inner healing and cleansing. He can make you pure again! Or if you're in a relationship that is rapidly heating up toward sexual compromise, God can strengthen you to reorder the boundaries of your relationship and preserve your purity.

Should you find yourself sorely tempted in your mind by a beautiful shapely woman or a handsome well-built man (not necessarily even their own doing), God can empower you to resist, despite your urges, and so remain faithful to your commitment to Him and to your spouse or family.

Jesus is coming soon, and I believe his promise is still true: "Blessed are the pure in heart, for they shall see God!" (Matt. 5:8, NKJV).

---

[1] Bob Smithouser, "Teen Romance Runs Aground" (a review of *Titanic*), *Plugged In,* 1998. See also www.fotf.org/goodread/a0000958.html.

[2] "The narrative has punctuated the imperative grammatical construction with raw power: *Lie with me*. As a servant Joseph must deal more with the reality of power than the danger of sexuality. . . . Joseph has said 'no' to one with power to destroy him and eventually must pay the consequences" (E. F. Roop, *Genesis*, p. 257).

[3] E. G. White, *Patriarchs and Prophets*, p. 214; italics supplied.

[4] Diane Hemphill McDonald, "Mom, What's Monicagate?" *Newsweek*, Mar. 9, 1998, p. 13.

[5] G. A. Getz, *Joseph*, p. 59.

[6] "Adultery: A New Furor Over an Old Sin," *Newsweek*, Sept. 20, 1996, pp. 54-60.

[7] E. F. Roop, *Genesis*, p. 257.

[8] White, p. 214.

[9] *People Weekly*, February 1997.

[10] Heinrich Heine, "The Lorelei."

[11] Dietrich Bonhoeffer, *The Cost of Discipleship* (New York: Macmillian Pub. Co., 1963), p. 148.

CHAPTER 6

Living on the Ragged Edge

GENESIS 39:7-23

A few winters ago my sons were absorbed in a snowball fight in the backyard. The snow that day was just right for forming white grenades that would explode wonderfully upon impact. And there was plenty of it. One could easily grab a handful of flakes and quickly transform them into smooth missiles to lob against foes. As snowball fighters often do, they were busy ducking shots and chasing each other down for point-blank shots in the back of the neck.

Somewhere along the way they got the idea of shooting at targets moving behind sliding glass doors. One boy had gone inside and was standing in full view through the doors that opened onto the back deck. Someone slammed a snowball at his image through the glass, but it merely exploded against the clear pane. This was fun! So he moved again and again, back and forth behind the glass doors, while his brothers tried to score. Each miss exploded on the sliding glass doors. Slushy gobs of white snow slowly sliding downward covered the glass.

Then suddenly an eerie snap cracked above their laughter. Jagged cracks shot out from the point of impact. Bit by bit one of the glass doors shattered into a million pieces, creating a spider's web of fragments. Everything viewed through that fragmented window was now blurred and distorted. Fragmented glass hinders clear vision.

Cry of the Soul

Joseph's sudden change of fortune and cruel imprisonment was like a careening snowball splintering the window of his heart. Now

God was not so easy to see. The view that had been so sharp suddenly changed. It was hard to see God through the pain and the fragments of hurt.

Listen to the psalmist's account of the kind of shock and pain Joseph experienced when he found himself cruelly imprisoned for being faithful to God and conscience: "He sent a man before them, Joseph, who was sold as a slave. They afflicted his feet with fetters, he himself was laid in irons; until the time that his word came to pass, the word of the Lord tested him" (Ps. 105:17-19).

Here you have the psalmist referring to Joseph being thrown into jail, fetters fastened around his legs so tight it hurt him. An interesting reading of the "he himself was laid in irons" renders it "an iron collar clamped on his neck" (NEB). Others simply say "his neck was put in irons" (NIV). But the Hebrew literally reads: "Into iron came his soul." The Hebrew word in this phrase for soul is *nephesh,* which includes more than mere body. It stands for the whole person, including one's emotions, feelings, and thinking. Rather than using one of the standard Hebrew words for "neck"—i.e., putting his "neck" in iron—Scripture says the Egyptians placed his "soul" in iron. It's an invitation to look deeper, to catch the heart of Joseph's prison experience. We're to envision more than physical restraint. Joseph's abusive confinement included his emotions and feelings. Yes, iron shackles cause serious bruises and wounds, but they injure the soul as well. This passage tells of damaged emotions, a crushed spirit, and a battered faith.

When the guards thrust Joseph into that dungeon and chained him so tightly that his feet ached, you can be sure his soul literally cried out in anguish. It wasn't just his body that felt pain.

Stepping back into Genesis for a moment, we can catch a further glimpse into Joseph's world of feelings. There in that prison house Joseph proclaimed his innocence to the soon-to-be-released cupbearer and asked for help. "Only keep me in mind when it goes well with you, and please do me a kindness by mentioning me to Pharaoh, and get me out of this house. For I was in fact kidnapped from the land of the Hebrews, and even here I have done nothing that they should have put me into the dungeon" (Gen. 40:14, 15).

First, Joseph proclaims his innocence as he feels the sting of injustice. He hasn't done anything to deserve his imprisonment. Second, he asks for a kindness. Not happy where he is, he pleads for help. Third, he calls the place a "dungeon." Up till then Genesis has used the word "prison." But when you hear Joseph talk about where he is, he calls it a dungeon. The Hebrew word means "pit"—the same word used earlier to describe where Joseph's brothers threw him (Gen. 37:20, 24). In other words, he considered his place of confinement a "miserable hole." When you are in a miserable hole, its hard not to feel miserable.

Psalm 105 lends still another important insight into Joseph's heart during this glass-shattering experience that blurred and distorted God's face. We find it in the phrase "until the time that his word came to pass, the word of the Lord tested him" (verse 19). Something that Joseph must have believed about God's word suddenly came under question. Maybe it was the dream he'd had years ago about being a ruler. Or perhaps it was God's promises—that if he followed and was obedient and faithful to Him, the Lord would bless him. Now not only wasn't he blessed; he was experiencing the exact opposite of what one might expect from obedience to God. What had become of all His promises to the faithful and obedient? In other words, Joseph was tempted to doubt the truth of the dream-promise. In the gloom of that miserable hole it was hard for him to believe in God's faithfulness and promised blessing, especially when his afflictions had come as a direct result of his obedience to God. *What have I gained from my integrity, my faithfulness, my purity, my obedience?* he must have wondered. *This is not fair!*

The book of Psalms reveals how Joseph's greatest trial had to do with trusting God's word when his soul was aching and crying out for help and his faith was being battered. More than imprisonment or pain, he struggled with the question of God and what He had said.

In life's ragged-edged moments, it is God's word that tries us the most. Not the experience we are going through, but what God promises for us when we go through them. Is that not really all we actually have to go on when the going gets rough—words? Everything we see, hear, experience, or think is ultimately translated into words in one way or another. Trials put our faith in God's words to the test.

Something about trials draws us back to the basics. Invariably, especially during a time of intense struggle, we return to our theological roots—back to God's Word. "Is it trustworthy?" we ask ourselves. "Is He trustworthy?" Quickly we find ourselves asking fundamental questions: "Who is this God who allows me to suffer such stuff? What is He up to now? How can I hang on? Where is God when I hurt so bad again and again and again? Can I still believe His Word? Can I still trust my life to Him?"

Just as shattered glass hinders our vision, so when we look for God through our pain and our hurt sometimes we just can't seem to see Him. And if we do catch a glimpse of Him, our pain and hurt and sorrow and loneliness—our aching soul—only distorts our view of God. The image standing behind that fragmented glass confuses us. This piece enlarges God and that one diminishes Him. Lines jigsaw their way across His face. Large sections of shattered glass block Him out altogether.[1]

And so we find ourselves parroting the ancient psalm:

> "Will the Lord reject forever?
>   Will he never show his favor again?
> Has his unfailing love vanished forever?
>   Has his promise failed for all time?
> Has God forgotten to be merciful?
>   Has he in anger withheld his compassion?"
>   (Ps. 77:7-9, NIV).

It is a fitting picture of the pit of discouragement. To be in that pit is to be trapped in an apparent cycle of never-ending problems, personal difficulties, and emotional trauma. Endless miles of bad road, cloudy days, dark nights. Unbroken hurt and pain. The glass-shattering circumstances of life each thrust us into a miserable hole in which the face of God is no longer clear.

Prison Primer

Joseph experienced it all—injustice, oppression, ingratitude, abandonment, mistreatment, physical pain, emotional wounds, the haunting search for meaning, doubt, hopelessness, discouragement. During the first 30 years of his life Joseph probably experienced more injustice than any biblical character other than Jesus Christ. Once he hit the dungeon, I'm sure he thought it would never end. The most natural response to discouragement is to complain, blame God, or feel that being good does not pay. Joseph's attitudes and actions throughout the whole ordeal, however, were incredibly exemplary for one who had endured so much mistreatment.[2]

Ellen White tells us that Joseph's true character revealed itself in the midst of this injustice. It "shines out, even in the darkness of the dungeon. He held fast his faith and patience; his years of faithful service had been most cruelly repaid, yet this did not render him morose or distrustful. He had the peace that comes from conscious innocence, and he trusted his case with God. He did not brood upon his own wrongs, but forgot his sorrow in trying to lighten the sorrows of others. He found a work to do, even in the prison. God was preparing him in the school of affliction for greater usefulness, and he did not refuse the needful discipline. In prison, witnessing the results of oppression and tyranny and the effects of crime, he learned lessons of justice, sympathy, and mercy, that prepared him to exercise power with wisdom and compassion."[3]

We find three principles to live by in Joseph's prison experience.

First, we must not allow ourselves to wallow in discouragement and hopelessness or permit bitterness to capture our soul. That means getting a grip on our emotions and feelings and focusing our hearts on God's Word. We must not brood over our wrongs and hurts and disappointments, but continue on with life wherever we find ourselves. Genesis records that Joseph found favor in the sight of the chief jailer and in time received important responsibilities in caring for others (Gen. 39:22, 23). It tells me that Joseph had no scowl on his face, grumpy attitude, or bitter heart. Something shown out from within him. He chose an attitude of contentment and cheerfulness. We need to learn how to follow his example in whatever circumstances we may find ourselves (Phil. 4:11).

Second, we must open our hearts to the reality of God's caring presence and His gracious blessing—even in the midst of our most heartrending and discouraging experiences. No matter what it looks like around us, we must turn to God even more. Genesis unequivocally states that "the Lord was with Joseph and extended kindness to him. . . . The Lord was with him; and whatever he did, the Lord made to prosper" (Gen. 39:21-23). It was a repeat performance of his days in Potiphar's house. When his brothers scorned him and sold him into Egyptian slavery, God did not abandon him. And when Potiphar sent him to prison again, the Lord stayed by his side. God never forgot Joseph, nor did He leave him. Joseph opened his heart to that truth even though his shattered heart would not at first enable a clear view. He chose to believe the word of the Lord anyway. Here we catch a glimpse into the incredible truth of how God can bless us as much and in just the same way when our circumstances appear bleak as when they appear rosy. Outward circumstances do not make a good barometer for measuring God's blessing. God can bless us even when we're down and out.

In her book *When God Weeps,* Joni Eareckson Tada shares how when she raised questions about why God had allowed her to be forever paralyzed, "My questions . . . created a paradox: in the midst of God's absence, I felt his presence. I found him after I let go of what I thought he should be. My despair ended up being my ally because through it, he took hold of me."[4]

At the height of one of his own personal tests, Hudson Taylor expressed his response in these words: "It doesn't matter how great the pressure is. What really matters is where the pressure lies, whether it comes between me and God or whether it presses me nearer His heart."[5]

I believe we get a clear sense of it with Joseph. When it came to the pressures of that dungeon experience, the pit of discouragement, the pressures lay beyond him in a way that pushed him closer to God. It was a matter of choice to believe God and His word.

Finally, we must reach beyond our own experience to encourage others who are hurting and discouraged. F. B. Meyer writes that "there is no relief for heart sorrow like ministry to others."[6] Ellen White tells us that Joseph forgot his own sorrow by trying to lighten that of others (Gen. 39:22; 40:6, 7).[7] The pathway out of the pit of discouragement always leads by the side of others who also sorrow.

We find in Joseph's dungeon experience a picture of a person absorbed with God and the needs of others. The way through the pit of discouragement is a conscious choice to believe God's Word and open our hearts to His promised presence. It includes compassionate ministry to others. Despite the shattered glass, we still discern not only God's face but also the face of others.

"Dark days call for right thinking and vertical focus,"[8] Charles Swindoll said. "Whenever you get into a prison of circumstances, be on the watch. Prisons are rare places for seeing things,"[9] F. B. Meyer adds. We have the promise of seeing God in a new way and of finding that His Word is as true as He is. And we will understand that from the anguish we have gone through God wants to bring compassionate support to other hurting people (2 Cor. 1:5-7).

Joseph prospered even as his life touched bottom and he descended further into difficulty. He did not cave in to despair or bitterness, but opened his heart to humility and empathy as he served others hurting around him.

Who among us does not know what it means to be misunderstood, misrepresented, accused falsely, punished wrongfully, or beset by opposition, obscurity, or scorn? Who among us has not looked for God through a glass-shattered heart? What do you do when life jerks the rug out from under you? Do you panic? Become discouraged and doubt the Lord's love? Or do you trust in God to get you through tough times, believing that He will work all things together for good?

Joseph's experience assures us that we can trust God to be with us. That He will use us in those discouraging moments in which we find ourselves to be a blessing to someone else. "God's presence does not ensure that . . . life will be lived triumphantly day after day," but we can be sure He will be with us day after day.

---

[1] Imagery taken from Max Lucado, *In the Eye of the Storm* (Dallas: Word Pub. 1991), p. 107.

[2] G. A. Getz, *Joseph*, p. 73.

[3] E. G. White, *Patriarchs and Prophets,* p. 219.

[4] Joni Eareckson Tada and Steven Estes, *When God Weeps* (Grand Rapids: Zondervan Pub. House, 1997), p. 155.

[5] As quoted by Charles R. Swindoll, *Hope Again: When Life Hurts and Dreams Fade* (Dallas: Word Pub., 1996), p. 212.

[6] F. B. Meyer, *The Life of Joseph,* p. 46.

[7] White, p. 218.

[8] Charles R. Swindoll, *David: A Man of Passion and Destiny* (Dallas: Word Pub. 1997), p. 118.

[9] Meyer, p. 45.

[10] E. F. Roop, *Genesis,* p. 256.

CHAPTER 7

"I Dreamed of Fat Cows on the River Nile"

GENESIS 41:1-16

I dreamed of seven sleek fat cows grazing on the river Nile, but I don't know what it means." "I dreamed of seven gaunt cows on the river Nile eating up the sleek fat cows, but I don't know what it means." "I dreamed of seven full ears of plump grain growing on a single stalk, but I don't know what it means." "I dreamed of seven thin and scorched ears of grain swallowing up the seven plump, full ears, but I don't know what it means." "I'm in the dark." "I have no idea what's going on." "There's something I'm missing." "No one could explain it to me."

We can only imagine the emotion in Pharaoh's voice or the expression on his face as he anxiously recounted his dreams to Joseph. The imagery of weak things devouring the strong alarmed him. Pharaoh had no idea what it might mean. Genesis tells us that "his spirit was troubled" (Gen. 41:8), leaving him upset and worried.

The same had happened with Pharaoh's baker and butler. "I dreamed of squeezing grapes into Pharaoh's cup and putting the cup into his hand," the cupbearer told Joseph. "But I don't know what it means."

"Yeah, I dreamed that birds were eating bread from three baskets that were stacked on my head," the baker chimed in. "But I don't know what it means." They, too, felt stumped and worried. Nor did they at first have anyone to interpret for them, either. In time Pharaoh asked his magicians and wise men—all the intellectuals and sages of Egyptian society—to weigh in with their insights.

They, too, came up empty. Butler, baker, Pharaoh, magicians, wise men of the land—all were in the dark.

After all, who on the face of it could have discerned the meanings of any of these dreams? If the butler had told you his dream, would you have known its meaning? How about Pharaoh's dream? Would you have figured that one out? No one knows their dreams' significance until Joseph interprets them. Even we don't!

It's a curious story with an absolutely simple plot. Only Joseph senses the course of the future. He alone recognizes the obvious meanings of things while everybody else is in total darkness.[1] That became true later even with his brothers. Only Joseph could discern between good and evil and spot God's providential hand. Pharaoh ultimately conceded that very point when he said, "There is no one so discerning and wise as you are" (verse 39). No one can grasp what Joseph does.

So Joseph interprets. As he does so, he points toward a generation of God's people who both discern the times and have spiritual insight to understand what's really going on in the world. The story of Joseph foreshadows those who both follow God and are able to grasp the larger meaning of world events. God had Genesis written for a generation of His people who had wandered in the wilderness and were now poised to enter the Promised Land. As we come to the close of Genesis, Joseph stands out as a paradigm of the character and the kind of people whom God would prepare to experience that Promised Land. One of those characteristics that Joseph models is the ability to grasp the issues at stake. People who will grasp the values at issue in the last days and who can articulate a clear way for others to follow safely. They can explain the meaning of Bible prophecy.

Many today are just like Pharaoh—in the pit of ignorance. They have little insight into the significance of what takes place either in their own personal lives or in the larger world around them. Unaware of the issues, they have no idea where things are headed or the true significance of whatever our postmodern culture tries to convince them is important.

Many in our world today have troublesome visions of weak things devouring the strong—a sense that all is not well. But they don't know what exactly it is that's wrong or why. They have a hard time sorting through the right and wrong of moral issues.

I find that even in Adventist circles. More and more I find people asking, "What is wrong with this?" or "Why can't I do that?" While there's nothing wrong with asking questions, it does tell me it is time for us to do some thinking. We need to ascend, as individuals, congregations, and as a church, out of a pit of ignorance on the moral and spiritual issues around us.

A God-dominated Imagination

Joseph's experience with Pharaoh is a story of spiritual discernment. The emphasis here on *good* and *bad* cows and *good* and *bad* ears of corn appears to stress the difference between *good* and *evil* and point to Joseph's ability to distinguish between the two. In doing so, Genesis artfully brings us full circle back to one of the central themes of its opening pages—"the knowledge of good and evil"—and that's the ability to discern between moral good and evil (Gen. 2:17; 3:5, 22).[2] Spiritual discernment—knowing the moral difference between good and evil—is crucial to life and happiness. We will note more fully later that it is clear from the story that such knowledge on Joseph's part comes only as a gift from God (Gen. 41:39). Here we simply want to show how, after sin entered our world, the issue of spiritual discernment became crucial. Genesis comes back to the point. Let's keep in mind the difference between "knowing good and evil" by experience, something undesirable in Genesis 2 and 3, and knowing it through moral/spiritual discernment as God's gift to those trusting Him, the point in view here.

In 1 Corinthians Paul point-blank tells us that spiritual things are spiritually discerned (1 Cor. 2:9-15). It's hard to accept, but it's true! We can look some things in the face all day long and still not grasp their true meaning. For example, we may feel that there are some things in Scripture or the writings of Ellen White that sound foolish or unimportant or outdated or legalistic. We may even be bothered or baffled by some claims of Scripture, the standards of lifestyle that it communicates to us, or the moral/spiritual values it expresses. Perhaps we may have a hard time with it. That's natural, the apostle Paul says. "Only those who have the Holy Spirit within them can understand what the Holy Spirit means. Others just can't take it in"

(1 Cor. 2:14, TLB). They just can't get it, because spiritual things are spiritually discerned.

Pharaoh rightly perceives what's going on when he declares to everyone in his court that Joseph is a man "in whom is the spirit of God" (Gen. 41:38, NIV). The book of Genesis refers only to Joseph as having God's Spirit in his life. And among the stories that Genesis more comprehensively develops, he is the only character who has an absolutely impeccable personal moral life.

If we want spiritual discernment, it demands two important qualities in our lives. Number one is an uncompromising moral integrity. And two, we must have a God-dominated imagination. We have already noted Joseph's untarnished and consistent path of moral integrity. The Bible does not accuse him of a single moral or spiritual compromise. The scriptural record contains no dirty laundry to hold up for us to gape at and exclaim, "Aha, he's no different than we are." No, you can't find it. I suggest that such a life of consistently following God's will, even in the small things, will build up a reservoir of moral orientation.[3] It will also give us a good supply of moral intention. Moral integrity stands behind spiritual discernment. They are like two sides of a coin, always together. Compromise in even the little things affects our ability to grasp deeper spiritual things. Moral compromise blurs moral insight.

Joseph's sterling character can be quite daunting in the face of our own experience. However, when we remember that his story starts in the pit of being human, the same place where every one of us stands, we can take courage from his example. We, too, can be overcomers— not in our own strength, but through God's incredible life-transforming power. The bottom line is choice. Joseph chose a consistent obedience, and so can we. When we do, God graciously works "both to will and to do of His good pleasure" (Phil. 2:13, KJV).

A couple years ago my family backpacked in Montana's Glacier National Park. During that trek we wished again and again for a pair of binoculars so we could see the wildlife better. When we got back to the campground we were staying at, I drove off to a sport shop to get a pair. There I found binoculars for $70, $150, $450, $870, even as high as $1,500. I hadn't imagined such a price spread, so I asked the man behind the counter, "What's the difference?" He lined up all the same-power binoculars in a row according to price and said, "Take a look. I will tell you how much they cost as you try each one." So I picked up the $70 pair. Things looked pretty good through them. Then I tested the $150 ones, and objects appeared even better through *them*. The $450 pair made things look great. "Whew, these are nice," I said when I gazed through the $870 pair. But when I picked up the $1,500 Zeiss binoculars, I said, "Oh, wow! I wish I could talk my wife into buying these!" It was incredible. The quality of the glass used as well as the grinding and polishing and coating put on it made all the difference. A cheap pair of binoculars gives the impression you are peering into a clouded world. A haziness blurs details and gives a sense of darkness. Grab those Zeiss glasses, however, and it's as if you can see a hundred miles.

That's what moral integrity enables one to experience—the ability to have enhanced, even correct, spiritual discernment and moral vision. If you have compromised your life in any way, you can be sure it will affect your ability to see and understand spiritual things.

When Joseph went before Pharaoh, Scripture tells us he shaved and changed his clothes (verse 14). Perfect cleanliness and proper dress were important in the eyes of the Egyptians. I believe the meaning reaches deeper, though. Joseph's clean-shaven face and spotless clothes said something about the impeccable moral quality of his life. His ability to interpret for Pharaoh was linked to his moral excellence and uncompromising life. If Joseph had not been so careful about moral and spiritual issues, he would never have been able to stand before Pharaoh and interpret the dream. Nor could he have outlined a wise response to that dream.

One of my sons went on a school field trip to the aviation museum in Kalamazoo, Michigan. It had a new flight simulator. Each one of the young people on the trip that day had the opportunity to get into that simulator and experience the excitement of flight. The experience absolutely awed my son. We had just purchased a flight simulator for our home computer, but it was nothing compared to the incredibly realistic graphics of the wraparound experience at the air museum. When he returned home he just overflowed with excitement and stories about what he had experienced and seen. The field trip had gripped his imagination, and his mouth gave spontaneous expression to what was bubbling up from within.

When anything catches our imagination, it gushes out naturally. I want us to see that the spontaneous way that Joseph spoke of God revealed a heart filled with Him. The Lord was on Joseph's mind, compelling him to speak of His Creator:

"It is not in me; God will give Pharaoh a favorable answer" (verse 16).

"God has shown to Pharaoh what He is about to do" (verse 28).

"The matter is determined by God, and God will quickly bring it about" (verse 32).

"Do not interpretations belong to God?" (Gen. 40:8).

When our heart is full of God, the tongue cannot help speaking of Him. Joseph clearly had a God-dominated imagination.

In his book *Leap Over a Wall* Eugene Peterson wrote: "The moment we permit evil to control our imaginations, dictate the way we think, and shape our responses, we at the same time become incapable of seeing the good and the true and the beautiful."[4]

As with Joseph, our generation needs to acquire a God-dominated imagination in the midst of a culture that would seek to impose an imagination dominated by evil. The distinction between the sacred and the common—between good and evil—have so blurred that it is no longer easy to grasp spiritual truth or moral truth. Evil has become so prevalent that it has become acceptable. It has become so much the norm that it no longer appears immoral. That's the grip of contemporary culture on our mind and heart.

Joseph, though, had immersed himself in the greatness and immediacy of God. Ellen White tells us that "the sights and the sounds of vice were all about him, but he was as one who saw and heard not. His thoughts were not permitted to linger upon forbidden subjects."[5] Rather, Joseph practiced the presence of God. Because He had so clearly fixed God in his imagination, he was still able to see the good and the true and the beautiful and the excellent even while living in an immoral, decadent culture. That's what God summons each one of us to experience.

Joseph did not have the advantage of either the Ten Commandments or the written Word as we know it today. Nevertheless his story is one of powerful spiritual and moral insight, incredibly deep by even our standards. He gained both spiritual discernment and moral orientation after years of faithfully doing what was right. If we faithfully do what is right, we also will build up a reservoir of moral orientation. When we link that with a God dominated imagination, we will have incredible moral and spiritual insight. A long-term obedience coupled with a God-dominated imagination can enable us to have tremendous spiritual perception.

"God has informed you," Pharaoh said (Gen. 41:39). Pharaoh acknowledged Joseph as a man "in whom is the Spirit of God" (verse 38, NIV). That is true! At bottom, we do not discover truth—God reveals it to us in the context of a personal relationship with Him.[6] God reveals Himself, His ways, and His purposes. We cannot know and understand spiritual or moral truth apart from His presence in our lives. If we want spiritual discernment, we must cultivate a love relationship with Him, yielding our lives to Him in faithful obedience.

We cannot discover the unknown or the future through an analysis of dreams or the crunching of texts or Ellen G. White passages. It comes only in the context of an intimate relationship with God and as a gift from God.

Thus while Joseph could discern between good and evil, the ability originated from God. Joseph's relentless commitment to the Lord is key. "The fear of the Lord is the beginning of knowledge" (Prov. 1:7). The Holy Spirit filled his heart and opened his eyes so that he became a wise interpreter.

Paul pointed to our need for this kind of experience when he wrote: "You have become dull of hearing. For though by this time you ought to be teachers, you have need again for some to teach you the elementary principles of the oracles of God, and you have come to need milk and not solid food. For everyone who partakes only of milk is not accustomed to the word of righteousness, for he is a babe. But solid food is for the mature, who because of practice have their senses trained to discern good and evil" (Heb. 5:11-14).

Spiritually mature, their senses trained to discern good and evil, is what God wants of His final generation of people. He longs to give us spiritual discernment for ourselves, for our families, for our churches, and for our dying world. It's time for us to ascend from the pit of ignorance and become wise and discerning interpreters for a world lost in darkness.

You're in Charge

What happens when we are faithful to God? When we live truth clearly, plainly? The same thing that Joseph experienced. Others will have hearts open to receive what we see and stand for. People will begin to trust themselves with us. They accept the hope and light and truth we bring in our own lives.

When Joseph first stood before Pharaoh, the Egyptian ruler said, "I've heard about you" (see Gen. 41:15). "You have a reputation of being able to solve deep things. And I'm in a mess. Please help me out." It's interesting that Joseph didn't just interpret Pharaoh's dream, but outlined a wise course of action as well. It is not enough for us to know the difference between good and evil, right and wrong. We must know what to do about these things as well. Issues always have a practical side to them. That's part of our mission—to outline a safe path for people to follow. And so we find Pharaoh turning everything over to Joseph. "You're in charge," he tells him, placing the whole Egyptian kingdom in his hands. His reaction tells me that when we are faithful to God and He dominates our mind, that fact will show in our lives. And people will trust us. They will listen to what we have to say about God, about the atoning work of Jesus on their behalf, about Sabbath, about standards, about the return of Jesus.

Biblical history casts Joseph in the role of a savior of his people. His practical insights save the Egyptians and ultimately his own family.

By the time he stood before the most powerful man in the world, Joseph already had a track record that inspired confidence in what God said. How about you? What kind of reputation do you have? Do people turn to you for insight? Trust you? Daniel 12:3 tells us that the wise will shine like the sun and win many souls.

After the devastating tornadoes that ripped through Alabama in the spring of 1998, I heard a radio interview with a single parent with two little children, who had lost absolutely everything. The reporter asked, "What are you going to do now?"

"I have no idea what I'm going to do now," came the reply. "I will trust myself and my life in the hands of those who know."

The mother of one of my wife's violin students was returning from a shopping trip when her Mazda MX6 suddenly burst into flames. Sherry was just driving along when the dashboard began emitting so much smoke that she couldn't see or breathe. She instantly hit the window buttons, sending the windows down. Then she stuck her head out the window to look for a safe place to pull over. Across the road a driveway led into a funeral home. So she yanked the steering wheel in that direction and pulled her car into the driveway and out of traffic. As soon as she stopped, Sherry burst out the door and around the car to get her 4-year-old son out of his car seat. But the seat belt buckle jammed. As more smoke billowed and the heat become more intense, she began to pray, "Lord, please help me, please help me!" After what seemed an eternity the buckle finally released, and she pulled her son from the flaming car. No sooner had Sherry stepped back than the flames and smoke completely engulfed the car. As she shared this incredible moment with me later, Sherry could only praise God for His gracious protection. And as I prayed with her, tears just welled up in her eyes at what might have been.

Our world plunges toward destruction, but many will make a last-moment escape. Why? Because God has used someone who understands Scripture and the issues. Someone who has a heart filled with a vision of God and whose life has a track record that others can't miss. Because of that kind of influence in their lives, they will make a decision for eternity.

---

[1] J. H. Sailhamer, *The Pentateuch as Narrative,* p. 212.

[2] *Ibid.,* pp. 215, 216.

[3] "There are few who realize the influence of the little things of life upon the development of character. Nothing with which we have to do is really small. The varied circumstances that we meet day by day are designed to test our faithfulness and to qualify us for the greater trusts. *By adherence to principle in the transactions of ordinary life, the mind becomes accustomed to hold the claims of duty above those of pleasure and inclination.* Minds thus disciplined are not wavering between right and wrong, like the reed trembling in the wind; they are loyal to duty because they have trained themselves to habits of fidelity and truth. By faithfulness in that which is least they acquire strength to be faithful in greater matters" (E. G. White, *Patriarchs and Prophets,* pp. 222, 223; italics supplied).

[4] Eugene H. Peterson, *Leap Over a Wall* (San Francisco: Harper San Francisco, 1997), p. 39.

[5] White, p. 214.

[6] Henry T. Blackaby and Claude V. King, *Experiencing God* (Nashville: Broadman and Holman Pub., 1994), pp. 56, 143.

CHAPTER 8

When Nobodies Become Somebodies and Somebodies Remain Nobodies

GENESIS 41:38-45

Thirteen years had elapsed since Joseph's brothers stripped off his colorful tunic and sold him to Midianite slave traders. During those years he had known intense heartbreak, bitter betrayal, exhilarating success, and crushing disappointment. Incredible temptation and unimaginable trial had ravaged him. But nothing compared to his meteoric rise from the dungeon to the position of prime minister of Egypt. Joseph's sudden promotion is overwhelming and almost breathtaking. One day he's a mere slave serving an open-ended prison sentence with no hope, status, or influence. The next day he receives the highest position in the Egyptian government—second only to Pharaoh himself.

The privileges, power, and prestige that went with his meteoric promotion accentuate why it was so dramatic and incredible. The record of what Pharaoh both said and did to Joseph that day is illuminating. It outlines the litany of an official Egyptian installation to high office and celebrity status.[1] If you were being promoted to high office in Egyptian culture, this is what you'd expect.

First, Pharaoh gives Joseph unrivaled and absolute political power. "You shall be over my house," he announced, "and according to your command all my people shall do homage; only in the throne I will be greater than you" (Gen. 41:40). "No one will make a decision regarding Egyptian affairs without your advice and approval," he added (verse 44, my paraphrase). Joseph thus became *the* prime mover and shaker in Egyptian political life.

The geographic extent of Joseph's political control and influence was immense. "See I have set you over all the land of Egypt," Pharaoh declared (verse 41). Egypt's vast fertile culture extended the length of the Nile.

In addition, Pharaoh gave Joseph sweeping financial authority. When the Egyptian ruler took off his signet ring and put it on Joseph's finger, he handed Joseph complete financial authority (verse 42). Egypt's wealth was limitless. Whenever Joseph impressed that seal on wax or ink or clay, he had control of the nation's finances. He could stamp any invoice, authorize any expenditures, enact any taxes, and pay any amount to carry out the king's business.

Joseph then acquired social prestige and untold royal privileges as well. He had all the trappings and perks of the prominent: the robes of fine linen, the gold chains, the grand chariots, the crowds shouting their adulation. Like any high government official, he had his own security force and advance public relations teams (verses 42, 43).

Finally, Joseph became a compelling religious icon. Pharaoh renames Joseph Zaphenath-paneah (verse 45). He also gives Joseph a wife from a high-ranking priestly family, the same family the pharaohs chose their wives from. Her name was Asenath (verse 45). Some have suggested that the term *nath* in both their names conveys the idea that "God speaks and lives."[2] Everything in Egyptian culture and reality revolved around religious themes and images. The sacred and the gods permeated everything. Together the celebrity couple represented not only the king of Egypt but deity as well. "Their names would constantly remind people of their religious position in the kingdom."[3]

Unrivaled political power, social prestige, untold royal privileges and perks—he had it all. Joseph had soared to the very summit of what it meant to live in Egyptian life and culture. You couldn't go any higher. The moment he reached that celebrated pinnacle, he found himself in another pit—prosperity!

Little People in Big Jobs

We have four boys in our home. At one time or another each has had the responsibility of pouring drinks at mealtime. Most of the time it goes quite well. But sometimes one of them has filled a glass past its brim. Somehow, when pouring the milk or juice, they either tipped the jug too much or they just weren't thinking about what they were doing. Anyway, the glass filled up fast—so fast they barely had time to yank the jug back in time. Too late, though. The cup was already full past the brim. But surprisingly, it didn't overflow. The milk or juice just kind of wobbled and shimmered, held together by surface tension. Everyone knew not to move or shake the table. Snickers grew as people held their breath. Then someone gently leaned down and sipped off the threatening spill.

In his book *Spiritual Manpower* J. Oswald Sanders writes, "Not every man can carry a full cup. Sudden elevation frequently leads to pride and a fall." According to Sanders, the most exacting test of all is prosperity.[4] Not every man or woman can carry a full cup!

Ellen White agrees. "One cannot stand upon a lofty height without danger," she writes. "As the tempest leaves unharmed the lowly flower of the valley, while it uproots the stately tree upon the mountaintop, so those who have maintained their integrity in humble life may be dragged down to the pit by the temptations that assail worldly success and honor."[5]

Prosperity carries its own temptations, its own challenges to our identity and our integrity. Our most difficult times are not when things are going hard. Hard times create dependent people. Survival keeps you humble. But when prosperity comes and you've just received that promotion or you're growing in prestige, fame, and success—that's the time to watch out. You're the most vulnerable when you feel the least accountable. Then you will lose your spiritual and moral concentration.

In his book *The Success Syndrome: Hitting Bottom When You Reach the Top,* Steven Berglas traces the pain and moral compromise that so often comes with prosperity. People hitting the top often reach bottom in their moral and spiritual life.

Solomon puts an interesting twist on all this when he writes, "I have seen slaves riding on horses and princes walking like slaves on the land" (Eccl.10:7). In other words, little people can wind up with big jobs. Fools are not limited to places of low esteem. Sometimes they become governors, legislators, even presidents! Or they can become principals of schools and pastors of churches. Nobodies can become somebodies but still remain moral and spiritual nobodies.

Joseph was a prime candidate for pride, abuse of power, irresponsible behavior, and moral license. But the overall story of Joseph's life reveals that when he was a nobody, he was really a somebody. And when he became a somebody, he handled a "full cup" very well. Ellen White tells us Joseph's character bore the "test . . . of prosperity."[6]

Carrying a Full Cup

We cannot help asking again—as we have done from pit to pit in Joseph's experience—How did he do it? What made him different? How do we carry a full cup? What principles can we learn so that we won't hit bottom when we reach the top?

First, Joseph was God-poised rather than self-poised. William Taylor puts it succinctly: "The balance of his nature was God. That kept him always in equilibrio, so that he was still the same man in simplicity, humility, and calmness, whether he was ministering to the prisoners in the round house or riding in the second chariot of the king. God was with him in the dungeon, and that kept him from over-estimating its hardships; God was with him in the chariot, and that kept him from over-estimating its honour. The affliction did not sour his heart, and the prosperity did not turn his head, because in both he felt that God was near him."[7]

"I fear God," Joseph told his brothers when they came to him for grain (Gen. 42:18). He had a profound sense of being responsible to Him for what he did and the opportunities he received. Joseph was God-poised rather than self-poised.

Second, Joseph allowed himself no moral or spiritual holidays. In *My Utmost for His Highest,* Oswald Chambers has a reading called "The Relapse of Concentration." Here he traces the theme that we may be all right in general, but can occasionally become slipshod, losing our spiritual concentration: "You no more need a holiday from spiritual concentration than your heart needs a holiday from beating. You cannot have a moral holiday and remain moral, nor can you have a spiritual holiday and remain spiritual. God wants you to be entirely His, and this means that you have to watch to keep yourself fit."[8]

Prosperity breeds a holiday spirit, as do vacations and traveling and days off or when life slows down and we're not so busy. We find ourselves out of our routine. Away from accountable situations, we pray less and skip devotions. Surrounded with blessings and the good life, we often relax our spiritual and moral concentration and do little things we might not normally do. Take in that movie. Pick up that magazine. Go to that place of entertainment. But Joseph allowed no lapse of spiritual concentration, no moral or spiritual holidays.

He also grasped a bigger picture. Henry T. Blackaby and Claude V. King have coauthored a powerful book they've titled *Experiencing God*. It focuses on knowing and doing His will. One of their themes is the simple biblical truth that God is always at work around you, and He invites you to become involved with Him. God is not just sitting in some heavenly place passively observing whatever happens on earth, but is actively orchestrating history. As He redeems a lost world, He desires to involve His people in His salvational work. He calls us to watch for Him at work around us and to adjust our life so we can join Him wherever He is active.[9]

When Joseph became Egypt's prime minister God was guiding history and working to redeem a lost world. In His providence Joseph became the savior not only of Egypt, but a great portion of the ancient Near East, including the Hebrew nation. In the process Ellen White tells us, "Through Joseph the attention of the king and great men of Egypt was directed to the true God; and though they adhered to their idolatry, they learned to respect the principles revealed in the life and character of the worshipers of Jehovah."[10] She also states that "he fully believed that the divine hand had directed his steps, and in constant reliance upon God he faithfully discharged the duties of his position."[11] Given the unconditional trust Pharaoh placed in him—and in his God—"Joseph was under pressure to *not* fail his human master *or* his divine Master."[12]

William Taylor asks the burning question everyone raises about Joseph: "But why was he always doing his best? Because . . . if you care to read between the lines . . . he was always working for God."[13] Joseph grasped that bigger picture.

My wife and I were invited to participate in the interview process of a medical group in a nearby community. We had become quite close friends with two doctors and their wives who are Baptist Christians. They wanted to add another partner to their practice.

Men who were not in the least bit ashamed of their faith, the doctors had a burden for the lost around them and didn't hesitate to share Jesus when the opportunity opened. They were looking for another partner who would share their spiritual passion.

One candidate they had already interviewed was a self-proclaimed agnostic. Needless to say, our doctor friends shared the gospel with him and appealed to him to accept Jesus. He got out of there fast.

The candidate they invited us along to interview was a Seventh-day Adventist. They wanted both our input and for the Adventist doctor and his wife to feel at home and find a home as well. Much to our delight, the Adventist couple knew the Lord. During a prophecy seminar a year earlier both had found Jesus in a new and deeper way. They were growing Christians with a passion for Jesus and spiritual things. We had a wonderful evening, and our Baptist friends wound up hiring the Adventist doctor.

One part of our table conversation particularly interested me. One Adventist medical specialist already worked in this practice. But there was anger toward God and the church that created a spiritual distance and a self-proclaimed doubt about God. My Baptist friends were earnestly praying that their current Adventist employee would find Jesus. The Adventist doctor we were interviewing had already met the "fellow Adventist" and had the same burden for his spiritual awakening.

The bigger picture is always that God is at work redeeming a lost world. I must be a part of it. Genesis tells us that "Joseph went throughout the land of Egypt" (Gen. 41:45, NIV). Without doubt the passage indicates that Joseph began his work in his new position of authority by conducting a survey of the entire agricultural situation in Egypt. He likely gathered all the information that he would need for setting up storage for the gigantic food program he was responsible for. I imagine, though, that he was capturing a sense, too, of the gigantic work God must have in mind to redeem a lost pagan culture. Joseph saw himself as a player in a larger historical and spiritual movement that obliged him to use his God-given talents for the benefit of others.

Some time ago I spoke with a friend who was reflecting on some important ministry decisions in his life. They might very well catapult him into a larger sphere of influence and responsibility in God's work. As others examined his life to see if he had the right stuff, he himself wondered if he was up to it all. "You know," he said over the phone, "no matter how far I have come in ministry, or how much higher I might go in influence and responsibility—no matter what people think I am—I see myself as just a poor insignificant little boy with holes in his shoes playing in the fields where I lived with my family."

Naomi Rosenblatt tells how hard it was at first to maintain her identity when she came to the U.S. from Israel in the fifties. After she landed in New York with all its affluent consumerism she struggled to maintain the Spartan values she had been raised with. "No matter what our roots are," she writes, "if we develop an authentic personal identity early on, it will anchor us throughout our life."[14] Her mother used to tell her, "Even if you come from Timbuktu, if you know everything there is to know about Timbuktu you can travel anywhere in the world and never lose your way."[15]

It's like the mother of a young football player from a tiny town in Mississippi. Her son had just signed a lucrative contract with the NFL for more money than anyone in her family ever dreamed of. But she harbored no fears for her son and her family's identity. "I'll still keep this house. Fix it up, maybe, but this is where we live. None of us will change, because money can't change love. I firmly believe what I've taught all my boys: cherish the bridge that brought you across."[16]

"By the grace of God I am what I am," the apostle Paul would say. He knew all about Timbuktu. In reality he viewed himself as little more than an aborted fetus whose opportunities and privileges in life came only through the grace of God (1 Cor. 15:8-10).

When we rise from obscurity to prominence, or when we experience prosperity, the trappings of success threaten to supplant the values of our early life—the very values instrumental in helping us succeed. We can become so mesmerized by ourselves and our new situation that we lose touch with who we are and where we have come from.

Joseph always remembered his moral and spiritual roots. On his deathbed he appealed to his family to take his embalmed body with them when they returned to the land of promise: "And Joseph said to his brothers, 'I am about to die, but God will surely take care of you, and bring you up from this land to the land which He promised on oath to Abraham, to Isaac and to Jacob.' Then Joseph made the sons of Israel swear, saying, 'God will surely take care of you, and you shall carry my bones up from here'" (Gen. 50:24, 25). Joseph was "a great man who, in the glory of his exaltation, did not outgrow the simplicity of his youth."[17]

When we know all there is to know about Timbuktu, we can go anywhere in the world and not lose our way. And when we know all there is to know about our real identity—who we really are—we'll never get lost.

There we have it: God-poised rather than self-poised. Absolutely no moral or spiritual holidays allowed. Seeing the bigger picture of what God is doing in the world and wanting to be a part of it. Remembering who we really are without God's blessing.

That's what it takes to ascend from the pit of prosperity!

The most difficult test of all is prosperity. Not every man or woman can carry a full cup. And yet, nothing honors God more than faithfulness during times of prosperity.

We live in an age in which prosperity reigns. Each of us experience blessings in one form or another. In our own sphere we have prosperity, power, prestige—at home, church, work, in the community. The same God who enabled Joseph to ascend from the pit of prosperity helps us to bear the test for Him as well.

God is seeking to make somebodies out of nobodies. He seeks nobodies who, by His grace, will become genuine somebodies.

---

[1] Walter Brueggemann, *Genesis* (Atlanta: John Knox Press, 1982), p. 334.

[2] G. C. Alders, *Genesis* (Grand Rapids: Zondervan Pub. House, 1981), p. 216; G. A. Getz, *Joseph,* p. 104.

[3] Getz, p. 104.

[4] J. Oswald Sanders, *Spiritual Manpower* (Chicago: Moody Press, 1970), p. 44.

[5] E. G. White, *Patriarchs and Prophets,* p. 222.

[6] *Ibid.*

[7] W. M. Taylor, *Joseph the Prime Minister,* p. 231.

[8] Oswald Chambers, *My Utmost for His Highest* (Uhrichsville, Ohio: Barbour and Co.), p. 76.

[9] H. T. Blackaby and C. V. King, *Experiencing God,* pp. 50, 65-78.

[10] White, p. 22.
[11] *Ibid.*
[12] Getz, p. 106.
[13] Taylor, p. 233.
[14] N. H. Rosenblatt and J. Horwitz, *Wrestling With Angels,* p. 351.
[15] *Ibid.*
[16] *Ibid.*
[17] Taylor, p. 227.

CHAPTER 9

If You Know Everything There Is to Know About Timbuktu

GENESIS 41:38-45

Joseph wore jewelry! Did you catch that?

At the end of that mind-boggling day—in which he went from being a mere slave to prime minister of Egypt—we find Joseph wearing a magnificent ring, an elegant necklace of gold, and some of Egypt's finest linen clothes, and driving around in an ornate chariot (Gen. 41:42, 43).

Do you think he took that stuff off the next day? Gave it back to Pharaoh, saying, "I can't wear this. I'm a servant of the living God of heaven." Absolutely not! They were functional symbols of Joseph's new status and power in Egypt. But those functional symbols raise the ever-burning question of cultural assimilation. Joseph's meteoric rise to power completely encapsulated him in Egyptian reality. In one day he soared to the very top of what it meant to live in Egyptian life and culture. As a follower of the living God of heaven, how far should he go? Was it all right for him to wear jewelry or participate in other tangible Egyptian cultural idioms? How far can God's people go in following the physical cultural expressions of their day and yet remain distinct, pure, a living witness?

How did Joseph wend his way through the pit of cultural assimilation?

Did you know that some have appealed to Joseph as an example for wearing jewelry?[1] He's an illustration, they say, that the Bible never prohibits adornment in itself, only its promiscuous use. They will add that our official position of advocating the nonusage of jewelry is both unbiblical and cultural. That the Bible teaches moderation, not nonusage.

If Joseph, with his impeccable moral and spiritual character, could wear jewelry, why can't we? If we put on Joseph's colorful robe and dream of being a people as faithful as he, why can't that glorious vision include rings and necklaces? Doesn't Joseph's very example prove that character, not externals, is what is really important? If you've got the character, can you put on the hardware?

Without doubt we live in a time when more of us than ever are struggling with the rationale for our Adventist positions on jewelry and other lifestyle issues. The church today faces a real dilemma in the area of lifestyle standards. Confusion reigns as to what the Bible and the writings of Ellen White really say on lifestyle issues and what we call Christian standards. We find inconsistency in how we apply biblical principles and values. Some advocate legalism and others fear its influence.

When young people perceive our positions as inconsistent and unreasonable—not applicable to life at the beginning of the twenty-first century—they particularly leave the church and turn elsewhere. Eugene Peterson notes that the trend today is for the values and living styles of the youth to be pushed upward to the adult world: "Each generation is, in poet John Berryman's words, 'unwell in a new way.' The way in which the present generation is unwell—that is, the forms under which it experiences sin—is through episodes of adolescence. There was a time when ideas and living styles were initiated in the adult world and filtered down to youth. Now the movement goes the other way: lifestyles are generated at the youth level and pushed upward. Dress fashions, hair styles, music, and morals that are adopted by youth are evangelically pushed on an adult world, which in turn seems eager to be converted. Youth culture began as kind of a fad and then grew into a movement. Today it is nearly fascist in its influence, forcing its perceptions and styles on everyone whether he likes it or not."[2]

Communicating biblical values and positions to young people in a meaningful way is especially challenging. One of the arguments that never goes away is the question of culture. It seems that people today downplay all the significant passages of Scripture on lifestyle issues as being either cultural in nature or not saying all we have thought they did. The same goes for the writings of Ellen White. Many regard her writings as culturally oriented, dated, incomplete, and legalistic. People are looking for Christ-centered standards based on sound biblical principles. Unfortunately, for many, any appeal to Scripture for concrete injunctions and specific commands on lifestyle issues seems more like advocating legalistic rules.[3] That leaves the question of application open and elusive.

Since some have used Joseph as an example of jewelry usage, and because jewelry is viewed so much as a cultural issue, I want to employ it here as an example of how Joseph likely related to the varied cultural pressures of his day. As I do, I want us to keep in mind a broader spectrum of Seventh-day Adventist Christian lifestyle issues. I'm not just talking about jewelry or ornamentation as such, but raising the question How tangible does Christian living get in contemporary culture? How Egyptian did Joseph look? We will never know. But Joseph does present an example of a consecrated people in which external forms make a difference.

All About Timbuktu

In the previous chapter we learned how hard it was for Naomi Rosenblatt to maintain her identity when she first came to the United States from Israel in the fifties. She landed in New York with all its affluent consumerism and struggled to maintain the Spartan values she had grown up with. The seductive display windows of Saks, Tiffany's, and Bergdorf's constantly lured her to embrace the culture around her. "No matter what our roots are," she writes, "if we develop an authentic personal identity early on, it will anchor us throughout our life."[4] Her mother used to tell her, "Even if you come from Timbuktu, if you know everything there is to know about Timbuktu you can travel anywhere in the world and never lose your way."[5]

We learned that one reason Joseph withstood the test of prosperity was that he knew everything there was to know about Timbuktu. As long as he remembered certain things about his past— who he was—the pit of prosperity had no power over him. The same would be true with cultural assimilation. As long as Joseph clung to everything there was to know about Timbuktu, he could not lose his way in a pagan culture.

What was Joseph's Timbuktu? What did he know about it that kept him from losing his way in the midst of Egyptian culture? When Joseph harked back to his past, what were the values that carried him through Egyptian moral and spiritual values? Part of Timbuktu for Joseph was a solemn moment of family spiritual revival and consecration. We read about it in Genesis 35: "Then God said to Jacob, 'Arise, go up to Bethel, and live there; and make an altar there to God, who appeared to you when you fled from your brother Esau.' So Jacob said to his household and to all who were with him, 'Put away the foreign gods which are among you, and purify yourselves, and change your garments; and let us arise and go up to Bethel; and I will make an altar there to God, who answered me in the day of my distress, and has been with me wherever I have gone.' So they gave to Jacob all the foreign gods which they had, and the rings which were in their ears; and Jacob hid them under the oak which was near Shechem" (verses 1-4).

One gets the sense that it was no ordinary time in the life of Jacob and his family. Jacob's only daughter, Dinah, had gone off to visit the daughters of the land (to check out a little of contemporary culture of her day) and was raped by Schechem, the son of Hamor the Hivite (Gen. 34:1, 2). That all ended with Simeon and Levi vengefully slaughtering and looting an entire city (verses 25-29). Jacob's family was on a fast track toward moral and spiritual ruin. But God intervened! He called Jacob's family to an experience of worship. "Arise, go up to Bethel, and live there; and make an altar there to God, who appeared to you when you fled from your brother Esau" (Gen. 35:1).

In his heart Jacob knew that he and his family could not come before God in worship while pagan influences so filled their lives. *Patriarchs and Prophets* tells us that "with deep emotion Jacob repeated the story of his first visit to Bethel, when he left his father's tent a lonely wanderer, fleeing for his life, and how the Lord had appeared to him in the night vision. As he reviewed the wonderful dealings of God with him, his own heart was softened, *his children also were touched by a subduing power;* he had taken the most effectual way to prepare them to join in the worship of God when they should arrive in Bethel. 'And they gave unto Jacob all the strange gods which were in their hand, and all their earrings which were in their ears; and Jacob hid them under the oak which was by Shechem.' "[6]

It was a moment of family spiritual renewal with heartfelt consecration and worship. Joseph had been there as an impressionable lad, touched by that same subduing power. What did he learn that day as he witnessed firsthand his father's moving testimony and then his big brothers and aunt and mother and stepmothers—each removing certain garments and idols and pieces of jewelry from their lives in an act of consecration and worship? Two things!

First, the experience touched Joseph's young mind with the reality that the artistic expressions of a culture that people are so inclined to wear and adorn themselves with are *value-laden*. They express moral or spiritual significance that the wearers wittingly or unwittingly identify with. Their sense of self, value system, and view of God is somehow locked up in such concrete expressions.

Second, Joseph discovered that genuine consecration to God finds tangible expression in shedding those cultural idioms that convey ungodly values. Consecration to God includes external forms. While you can have the external forms in your life without consecration, you cannot have consecration without its affecting the external forms that in one way or another compete with that very consecration. Doing and being are inseparably linked. Here was the Timbuktu that kept Joseph from losing his way in the Egyptian world of incredible artistic cultural expression—expressions laden with pagan values and ideals.

The 1998 Andrews University Alumni weekend featured the unveiling of Alan Collins' bronze sculpture depicting the dauntless John Nevins Andrews family, Adventism's first missionaries, as they stood dockside in Boston in 1874, preparing to depart for Switzerland. *Legacy of Leadership,* the sculpture is called. It shows J. N. Andrews and his two children, Charles and Mary, watching their incoming ship. It captures both the eagerness and apprehension the missionary family must have felt at this important moment in their lives. Many have sensed how it whispers mission, commitment, and sacrifice for a people whom God intends to touch the world for

Him. "My heart is wholly bound up in this work; I have no desire but to live in the service of God," Andrews said. I cannot describe it, but from the moment I first saw photos of the proposed bronze sculpture, I felt moved. Moved with a desire for the same kind of commitment to God. One sunny afternoon I stood before this artistic expression of leadership and mission. Tears welled up in my eyes as I thought of that dauntless family and all they experienced together for the Lord. There I thanked the Lord for their powerful legacy and recommitted my own life to being a faithful servant to come and go at the Lord's bidding.

Such tangible artistic expressions reflect the worldview of their author or culture and powerfully convey their moral and spiritual values and ideals. Anyone who has visited Egypt or museums featuring Egyptology cannot help coming away impressed with the sheer power of the ancient civilization's artistic expression. The culture had magnificent architecture, grand sculptures, impressive pyramids, and vivid reliefs and murals, most in stunning color. It was a civilization steeped in artistic expression. You could not live in Egypt without the incredible power of its integrated cultural message influencing you.

Now, it's one thing for the power of a given culture and its tangible expressions to be everywhere around us and all-pervasive in its influence. But it's another thing for us to bring to our body or life those very objects, behaviors, experiences, or icons. The moment we do, we identify with them. Their moral and spiritual values somehow attach to our inner private world. Culture is no longer objective—out there. Now it is internal. It is shaping us inside. We experience and come to own culture by participating in its forms.

Again, *Patriarchs and Prophets* has some interesting things to say at this point: "He [Joseph] was here exposed to temptations of no ordinary character. He was in the midst of idolatry. The worship of false gods was surrounded by all the pomp of royalty, *supported by the wealth and culture* of the most highly civilized nation then in existence. Yet Joseph *preserved his simplicity* and his fidelity to God. . . . The desire to gain the favor of the Egyptians *could not cause him to conceal* his principles. Had he attempted to do this, he would have been overcome by temptation; but he was not ashamed of the religion of his fathers, and *he made no effort to hide* the fact that he was a worshiper of Jehovah."[7]

Even in an environment in which culture supported false worship, Joseph preserved his simplicity. He openly worshiped the God of His people. Obviously, it meant Joseph's character, life, and lifestyle did not follow the cultural norms of Egyptian society. One could tell where the new prime minister stood by his lifestyle.

Psalm 105 tells us that when Pharaoh promoted Joseph, Joseph had command over all Pharaoh's princes and officials, and that "he taught the leaders how to use wisdom" (Ps. 105:22, CEV). *The Living Bible* reads: "At his pleasure he could imprison the king's aides and teach the king's advisors." I like *The Jerusalem Bible's* way of putting it: Joseph was "to train his officials as he thought fit and convert his elders into sages."

Joseph taught Pharaoh's leaders wisdom. We've learned how Joseph became Egypt's prime shaker and mover and trendsetter. He was a compelling spiritual moral icon in a culture that encapsulated its religious and moral values in all the arts and sciences and everyday life. People looked up to him as possessing something different. Did he just go along for the ride, or did Joseph preserve and promote a radically different lifestyle?

Patriarchs and Prophets elaborates this very biblical theme: "Through Joseph the attention of the king and great men of Egypt was directed to the true God; and though they adhered to their idolatry, *they learned to respect the principles revealed in the life and character* of the worshiper of Jehovah."[8]

Character has to do with heart, demeanor, attitude, personal ethos, and temperament. Life consists of concrete external expressions of what resides in the heart and tangibly flows out from one's inner private world of being. Not only did Joseph's character express godly principles; they were tangibly expressed in what he said, what he ate, how he dressed, and what he did. Being and doing together wonderfully reveal truth about God and what it means to be His servant.

Let me suggest something. The Old Testament tends to devalue the significance of jewelry as a symbol of ultimate value.[9] Wisdom literature, such as the books of Proverbs, Job, and Psalms, contrast wise instruction with silver and gold and precious jewels:

"How blessed is the man who finds wisdom, and the man who gains understanding. For its profit is better than the profit of silver, and its gain than fine gold. She is more precious than jewels; and nothing you desire compares with her" (Prov. 3:13-15).

"Take my instruction, and not silver, and knowledge rather than choicest gold. For wisdom is better than jewels; and all desirable things can not compare with her" (Prov. 8:10, 11).

"There is gold, and an abundance of jewels; but the lips of knowledge are a more precious thing" (Prov. 20:15).

Egyptian civilization was a culture steeped in artistic expression. Its people used jewelry and other personal adornment to depict the principles of its religious and moral life. In his book *Jewels of the Pharaohs,* Cyril Aldred writes that men and women alike wore personal adornment and that even the gods had their jewelry too. The occupation of jeweler was one of the most flourishing in ancient Egypt throughout its long history.[10] Egyptian ornamentation expressed the civilization's cultural, social, religious, and magical practices and convictions. My own visit to Egypt startled me with this realization. You cannot miss it! Bracelets and pendants. Earrings and necklaces. Rings and earplugs. Amulets and headbands and anklets. The list goes on and on. Each work an incredible artistic expression with brilliant aesthetic color and appeal. And each an iconic depiction of some Egyptian god or religious concept. Gold was used frequently. As gold never lost its luster, but seemed to retain within itself all the fire and glory of the sun, the Egyptians felt that the flesh of the gods themselves must be made of this eternally shining material.[11]

I can just see Joseph—knowing all there was to know about his Timbuktu experience—teaching Pharaoh's leaders true wisdom. In one way or another, day after day he would devalue what lay at the very heart of their religious and moral experience and expression. Adornment depicted the individual Egyptian's interests, values, concerns, and fears. It was a concrete expression of his or her standing in society and before the gods. Have you ever had someone—whether male or female—tell you that they felt naked without certain forms of adornment, cosmetics, or garments on? That's how the Egyptian people would have reacted—completely vulnerable and naked without their ornaments. But Joseph's life and character and convictions and wise instruction would steadily devalue these very things in their eyes. As they watched his life they would always find themselves confronted by something vastly better.

What happens when you devalue things? They become less important, and in the process they lose their attraction and drop away.

When Debbie came to church for the first time she was wearing a white mink coat and was decked to the hilt with jewelry, cosmetics, and all that goes with it—shoes, purse, dress, hairstyle. Debbie was a jet-set yuppie real estate agent whose wild parties featured cocaine served in tiny silver cups and snorted through $100 bills. Driving fancy cars and living in a big house, she had it all. Studying the Bible with Debbie and her husband, Rick, was a real experience, to say the least. But here she was, her first Sabbath in a Seventh-day Adventist church and in my pastor's class. My congregation at that time was a friendly bunch who knew how to make people feel at home, and so in time Debbie merged right into our church life, where she laughed and fellowshipped and worshiped. No one to my knowledge ever spoke to her about her adornment and extravagant lifestyle. At least I know I didn't.

I'll never forget the day she asked me for baptism. *She needs some more time,* I thought to myself as she stood there wearing as much jewelry as ever. But I said, "Sure! When would you like to plan it?"

"This Sabbath," she replied.

"OK," I said with a bit of hesitation. "When can we meet to review a couple things?"

The only time that week Debbie had free was an hour before Sabbath school started, the day of her baptism. I knew she was up on all the things we had studied, so I wasn't too worried. Except, that is, for my chosen style of relating to certain lifestyle issues—let the Spirit lead in His way and in His time. Through the years I have learned that we need to give people space to grow at their own pace. Lifestyle issues need incubation time in each person's heart. You can't expect everyone always to read off the same page. And furthermore, people will make a decision on an issue, then fall back to where they were previously. They go up and down. It happens with longtime members as well. The only place the line needs to be clearly drawn is for leadership. Leaders in the body of Christ must set the pace toward that biblical ideal of a truly Christ-centered standard in which Spirit-filled hearts and a passionate love for Jesus compel obedience in unequivocal and tangible ways. No leader in the body of Christ has the right to interpret or project lifestyle issues from their own perspective. They have the responsibility to engender the lifestyle our world community has envisioned together.

I'll always remember that Sabbath morning meeting with Debbie on her baptism day. When she arrived she was dressed smartly, but gone were the cosmetics and fancy jewels that I had been accustomed to seeing her wear. It startled me, to say the least. She still looked lovely, but considerably different. I wanted to say something about it right off, but bit my tongue. When the appropriate moment came in our sharing together, I asked her about her thoughts on adornment. Here was a women who had been abused, gone through divorce, used drugs, and seen her brother carted of to jail for selling drugs. You name it, and she had been there or done that. "Pastor Larry, I don't need those things anymore," she replied. "What I want and what I need most is in that water."

What happens when the love and claims of the living God become all-absorbing? Tangible cultural expressions that compete with that vision become devalued and less important, then drop off. Whether it's personal adornment, questionable styles of music, media experiences, the kind of things we read or watch, recreational pursuits, whatever. Many of the tangible things representing our contemporary culture will lose their hold on us when a relationship with God becomes our all-consuming passion. When we love Him supremely and spend time in His word and fill our hearts with the guidance He has given us in the writings of Ellen White.

But Joseph still wore jewelry. It's an undeniable fact that shouldn't really bother us much. The ornaments he wore were functional symbols of his status and power in Egypt. He was Pharaoh's deputy with Pharaoh's signet ring and the power to legislate.

Scripture affirms the difference between the ornaments Joseph wore as prime minister and those he could have worn for personal ornamentation. Did you know that the only persons the Lord ever prescribed jewelry for was the high priest (Ex. 28), and perhaps the crown on Israel's king? Even then the jewels were on the high priest's clothing rather than on himself. When he took off his garments, he removed the jewelry. It's a fine distinction, but an important one in distinguishing the difference between ornamentation used for communicating moral and spiritual truth and that worn for personal adornment. Scripture depicts jewelry as used for personal adornment,[12] as a form of currency,[13] for offerings,[14] as evidence of wealth,[15] to designate social status,[16] as symbols of power and authority,[17] as imagery for God's gracious redemption and our value in His sight,[18] for religious purposes,[19] and possibly to ward off evil powers and dangers, i.e., magic.[20] Scripture does not reject the use of jewelry altogether. But it does devalue and call into question its employment for personal adornment and for religious and magical purposes.[21] Scripture draws a direct connection between luxury in adornment and dress and idolatry.[22]

When we understand the difference between the contemporary culture of biblical times (the lifestyle, customs, and values expressed by the nations and peoples of the then known world), the culture of biblical characters (the lifestyle, the customs, and the values expressed in the lives of individuals knowing or representing God), and heavenly culture (the values and lifestyle that Scripture projects as the ideal and true and that which has been expressed most fully in the life of Jesus Christ), we can put much of what Scripture says on the subject in context. We can read between the lines better and understand that not everything God's people did represents what He would have had them do. All of us need to grasp the principles and the values that God's Word illuminates and carefully observe the concrete ways He calls for us to apply them. Such tangible expressions of obedience point in the direction we must continue to go as we develop a distinct ethos from that of our contemporary culture.

Since we're in Genesis, I cannot help wondering if Joseph understood that God didn't create humanity wearing adornment. Man and woman's original adornment was that he and she together were made in God's image.

Where's Grace?

As I wrote this chapter I could not help asking, "Where's grace?" When you stop to view Joseph's life and all we have seen of him thus far, it becomes clear that the question of adornment has nothing to do with the basis of salvation. Rather, it involves spiritual boundaries. If Joseph had compromised in one small area, we are told, or not clearly shown where he really stood on certain issues, he would have been overcome immediately.

Where's grace? We find it in the principles of life that Joseph came to understand. It appears in the way that concrete injunctions (rules) illustrate how principles apply. Grace reveals itself in the clarity of values expressed in tangible ways and in divine empowerment through faithfulness even in little things. No, this is not a question of salvation, but of witness, influence, perseverance, and standing out for God in a confused, dying world.

In the end Joseph is not an example of how someone looked, but of the concreteness of his values and how they affected and sustained his moral life and witness in a culture that would have absorbed him into itself. From Joseph's experience we learn that external forms can express genuine consecration to God. They can help maintain a unique identity in a world that would squeeze us into its mold. Externals can create boundaries that protect us from those experiences that would blur our understanding of what is good and steal away our innocence (Rom. 16:19). Best of all, externals can bring a living witness to the true God and a vision of a better, more abundant way.

But externals are always minimums. Genuine Christ-centered, principled living will always call for ever-deepening and even more tangible expressions that reach toward applications we never dreamed of until a new consistency flavors our whole character and life. As Oswald Chambers writes, "God always educates us down to the scruple."[23] Ellen White would agree: "We must come nearer to God, place ourselves in closer connection with heaven, and carry out the principles of the law in the minutest actions of our everyday lives in order to be spiritually whole."[24] We must never forget, though, that externals must always be linked with a genuine experience of the heart in order for them to be what they were for Joseph. In all our "doing" there must be authentic "being."

Samuel Bacchiocchi raises a final issue on this topic well. In his book *Christian Dress and Adornment* he writes: "To believe that our outward appearance is an index of *our* character does not give us the right to judge others by *their* outward appearance."[25] The paradox of Christian lifestyle, he notes, is that "we *dare not judge others* by their appearance, yet *we dare not become a stumblingblock to others* by our appearance. Though others cannot read our heart, they can read our clothes, hairstyle, makeup. Our outward appearance makes a powerful statement for Christ."[26]

That is true for any lifestyle issue we approach as an Adventist people. We can never escape this paradox.

The external expressions of culture that human beings naturally bring to themselves and into their lives are all value-laden in one way or another. Some of the moral or spiritual values they convey can be good, true to what it means to be human and true to the larger biblical perspective of human beings in relation to God. Others, however, are neutral. And some are unquestionably evil. While you can have the external forms in your life without consecration to God, you cannot have consecration without its affecting the external forms that in one way or another either nurture or compete with that very consecration. Christian moral and spiritual reality inseparably link doing and being. That's something Joseph learned well. It's a personal journey for sure. But "if you know everything there is to know about Timbuktu, you can travel anywhere in the world and never lose your way."

---

[1] Dennis H. Braun, "A Seminar on Adventists, Adornment, and Jewelry" (D.Min. proj., Andrews University Theological Seminary, June 1996), p. 17; Madelynn Jones-Halderman, "Adorning the Temple of God," *Spectrum,* December 1989, p. 50.

[2] Peterson, *The Contemplative Pastor* (Dallas: Word Pub., 1989), pp. 128, 129.

[3] Steve Case, ed., *Shall We Dance* (Riverside, Calif., La Sierra University Press, 1996); Gary Land, "Adventist in Plain Dress," *Spectrum,* December 1989, pp. 42-48; Jones-Haldeman, pp. 49-55; Charles Scriven, "I Didn't Recognize You With Your Ring On," *Spectrum,* December 1989, pp. 56-59; Braun, pp. 6-87.

[4] N. H. Rosenblatt and J. Horwitz, *Wrestling With Angels,* p. 351.

[5] *Ibid.*

[6] E. G. White, *Patriarchs and Prophets,* p. 206.

[7] *Ibid.,* p. 214. Italics supplied.

[8] *Ibid.,* p. 222.

[9] Angel Manuel Rodriquez, "Jewelry in the OT: A Description of Its Functions" (unpublished manuscript for the Biblical Research Institute, 1998), p. 20.

[10] Cyril Aldred, *Jewels of the Pharaohs* (London: Thames and Hudson, 1971), p. 14; See also Adriana Calinescu, ed., *Ancient Jewelry and Archaeology* (Bloomington, Ind.: Indiana University Press, 1996).

[11] Aldred, p. 15.

[12] 2 Kings 9:30; S. of Sol. 1:10, 11; Isa. 3:16-23; Jer. 2:32; 4:30; Eze. 16:11-15; 23:40; Hosea 2:13; 1 Tim. 2:9; 1 Peter 3:3; Rev. 17:4, 5.

[13] Gen. 24:22.

[14] Ex. 35:22; Num. 31:50, 51.

[15] Gen. 24:10, 22, 35, 53; Ex. 3:22; 11:2; 12:35, 36; 32:2-5; Job 42:11; Rev. 18:12.

[16] 2 Sam. 1:10; 2 Kings 11:12; Ps. 45:13, 14; 89:39; 132:18; Isa. 3:16-26; Eze. 16:10-13; 28:11-19; Rev. 17:4.

[17] Gen. 41:42; 2 Kings 11:12; Esther 3:10, 12; 8:2, 8, 10, 15; Dan. 5:29; Zech. 6:11-13.

[18] Isa. 61:10; Mal. 3:16-18.

[19] Gen. 35:2-4; Ex. 28; 35:20-22; Eze. 16:17.

[20] This use of jewelry and adornment may be somewhat inseparable from its use for religious purposes, but it does appear that some forms of personal adornment worn by biblical characters had magical connotations. See reference to "amulets" in Isaiah 3:20 and the "skillful enchanter" in Isaiah 3:3. "The presence of religious and magic jewelry in the catalog of Isaiah 3 indicates that the pride of the 'daughters of Zion' was not just based on their financial security and their beauty or on their social position but specially on the psychological security that religious and magical pieces of jewelry provided for them" (Rodriquez, pp. 17, 18).

[21] Gen. 35:2-4; Ex. 32; 33. See Rodriquez.

[22] Gen. 35:2-4; Isa. 3; Rev. 17:4.

[23] Oswald Chambers, *My Utmost for His Highest,* reading May 13, p. 97.

[25] Ellen G. White, *Testimonies for the Church* (Mountain View, Calif.: Pacific Press Pub. Assn., 1948), vol. 4, p. 75.

[25] Samuele Bacchiocchi, *Christian Dress and Adornment* (Berrien Springs, Mich.: Biblical Perspectives, 1995), p. 176.

[26] *Ibid.,* p. 177.

CHAPTER 10

Freeing Your Mind From Memories That Bind

GENESIS 41:46-52

Sandwiched in the middle of the story of Joseph's meteoric rise to power and his subsequent administrative success as Egypt's prime minister is the report of the birth of his two sons—Manasseh and Ephraim (Gen 41:51, 52). It's just two brief matter-of-fact verses that you can easily overlook if you're not careful. Most of us wouldn't think about this kind of detail when the plot appears to be leaping quickly forward to the next dramatic moment when Joseph's brothers reappear (Gen 42:1-7). Aren't the verses just part of the background? The kind of minutia useful for rounding out the story, but unimportant to the overall plot? How many of us, if asked to tell the story of Joseph, would remember to include the part about the birth and naming of his sons? Probably not many.

Obviously, they were two highly important moments in Joseph's life. Apart from the fact that the birth of sons would bring celebration in any Middle Eastern home, or that Jacob would later himself adopt the two boys into the family of Israel—Jacob claimed them as his own, telling Joseph that the rest of his children were his to keep (Gen. 48:1-6)—the passage provides rare insight into Joseph's private inner world. From the interpretation that he gave to his son's names we "learn something of the deepest feelings of his heart"[1]

"God has made me forget all my trouble and all my father's household" (Gen. 41:51).

"God has made me fruitful in the land of my affliction" (verse 52).

When I read these words, something becomes extremely clear. I realize that Joseph was a deeply sensitive man with feelings and emotions that were real and unavoidable. He was no mere moral machine mechanically making his way through a life of moral excellence without feelings and emotions. It's easy for us to study the life of someone like Joseph, who had an impeccable moral and spiritual character—no flaws, no reference at all in the whole of Genesis to even one piece of dirty linen—and feel that, unlike ourselves, they have it all together inside their private inner world. We can jump to the conclusion that such exacting moral integrity somehow means they had no feelings or emotions—just raw obedience no matter how they felt. We conclude that absolute faithfulness to God can come only from a moral machine. This passage, though, tells us that Joseph was just as human as any one of us—and the emotional pain he experienced must have been at times almost more than he could bear.

We catch glimpses into Joseph's private inner world in those verses in which he speaks of forgetting his troubles, forgetting painful family memories, and living in a land of affliction. Twice Genesis reports that Joseph turned away from his brothers to weep uncontrollably (Gen. 42:24; 43:30, 31). When Joseph saw his younger brother Benjamin for the first time in 15 years—his mother's only other son—he lost it. The memories of his mother and those childhood days playing with his little brother flooded his heart. It was a painful moment. Scripture tells us he "hurried out for he was deeply stirred over his brother, and he sought a place to weep; and he entered his chamber and wept there" (Gen. 43:30). Deeply stirred, he sought a private place where he could freely let his surging emotions release in a flood of tears. Entering his chamber, he cried his heart out. In other words, something was going on deep down inside himself. Joseph was in touch with his feelings and emotions. And he had to deal with it, even if it meant laying aside some official business for the moment.

How long was he gone? How hard did he cry? We'll never know. But we do know he cried long enough and hard enough that he had to wash his face before he could appear in public again. And he had to wait long enough to regain control before he could come back (verse 31). Later Genesis reports that Joseph wailed "so loudly that the Egyptians heard it, and the household of Pharaoh heard of it" (Gen. 45:2).

All this tells us that Joseph was a man who struggled with emotional turmoil in his heart. His emotions were real and unavoidable.

From the moment his brothers stripped off his ornamental robe and thrust him into a pit like a mere animal, Joseph found himself in the pit of painful memories. In it his wounded soul cried out for healing and peace. Joseph had things he wanted and needed to forget. Our passage today tell us that he came to a moment in his life during which he could lay some things aside, and when he did, he ascended from the pit of painful memories.

Painful Memories, How They Linger

Joseph, Scripture tells us, named his first son Manasseh, a play on a Hebrew word literally meaning "one who causes to forget." He then explained why he chose the name: "God has made me forget all my trouble and all my father's household" (Gen. 41:51). Now the burning question is What did Joseph mean? He's in touch with what's going on inside him, so what did he forget?

➤ Did he forget how his brothers hated him and couldn't speak to him on friendly terms? (Gen. 37:4, 5).

➤ Did he forget the day they stripped him of his ornamental robe—that robe his father had given him—called him all kinds of names, and brutally threw him into that pit? (verses 23, 24).

➤ Did he forget how they ate a meal while they left him there to perish from hunger and thirst? (verses 24, 25).

➤ Did he forget the horrible moment when they bartered with the Midianite merchants and the dreadful truth dawned on him that he was to be sold as a slave—a fate to be feared more than death itself? (Gen. 37:25-28).

➤ Did he forget the agony and terror that rushed through him as he pleaded with one brother and then another for help, but each turned away and none would listen? (Gen. 42:21, 22).

➤ Did he forget those numbing days as he trudged wearily over the desert roads bound for a strange land, leaving his family forever behind?

➤ Did he forget the dehumanizing Egyptian slave block on which the traders sold him like an animal to the highest bidder—Potiphar? (Gen. 37:36; 39:1).

➤ Did he forget the daily experience of sexual temptations by a seductive and sensuous woman? (Gen. 39:7-10).

➤ Did he forget her cries of rape when he ran away, refusing to violate his moral principles and his master's trust? (verses 11-19).

➤ Did he forget how angry Potiphar got and the unfair way his master treated him? Did he forget how roughly the prison guard treated him? (Gen. 39:19, 20; Ps. 105:18).

➤ Did he forget those long years in prison as an innocent man? (Gen. 40:14, 15).

➤ Did he forget the cupbearer's failure to remember him when restored to Pharaoh's right hand? (Gen. 40:14, 15, 23).

It's a long list! Joseph never forgot any of these painful, humiliating events! How could he? The details were indelibly etched in his mind. If anything had totally erased the painful events from his memory, the overall experience would have been of little value to his moral formation. Furthermore, if he had forgotten them, he wouldn't have mentioned his "trouble" and his father's household at Manasseh's birth. The only way Joseph could say that God caused him to forget the troubles of his past was for him to have kept remembering them.

What then did God cause Joseph to forget?

Before we answer that question, we need to understand the link that exists between memory, emotions, and feelings. It's not always obvious in our conscious thought, but our feelings and emotions and our memories are inextricably bound to each other.

Someone has said that "memory is the power to gather roses in winter." That speaks to the positive side of memories, the joyous aspect of good memories. Good memories can bring us happiness and a sense of balance when things aren't going well in our lives. I think of how Viktor Frankl's memory of his wife helped him cope with the dehumanizing pain of Auschwitz:

"My mind still clung to the image of my wife. . . . I didn't even know if she were still alive. I knew only one thing—which I have learned well by now: Love goes very far beyond the physical person of the beloved. It finds its deepest meaning in his spiritual being, his inner self. Whether or not he is actually present, whether or not he is still alive at all, ceases somehow to be of importance.

"I did not know whether my wife was alive, and I had no means of finding out (during all my prison life there was no outgoing or incoming mail); but at that moment it ceased to matter. There was no need for me to know; nothing could touch the strength of my love, my thoughts, and the image of my beloved. Had I known then that my wife was dead, I think that I would still have given myself, undisturbed by that knowledge, to the contemplation of her image, and that my mental conversation with her would have been just as vivid and just as satisfying. 'Set me like a seal upon thy heart, love is as strong as death.'"[2]

But memory is also the power to get scratched by thorns year-round. No matter how pleasant or good your experience may actually be, memory has the ability to find thorns in it. Memories are the experiences of whole persons as they remember something, not simply neutral brain-stored pictures of the past. Computer-like bytes of objective data. Our memories express a whole person, and they include feelings, emotions, attitudes, and even tendencies toward actions that accompany the pictures that flood the video screen of the mind. When Scripture refers to memory, it does not have in mind mental pictures but whole persons orienting all their thoughts and actions toward either embracing something or letting something go, whether it be an experience, an object, or some relationship. The Bible presents a wholistic idea of memory.[3]

Memory and feelings and emotions are inseparable. When something stirs up a memory, deep emotions and feelings usually accompany it. Our emotions connect our inner world to the ups and downs of our outer world. Sometimes the connection is more than we can bear. As a result we discover things that we want to avoid or ignore or forget altogether about our outer world—but they are still there in our inner world.

In their book *The Cry of the Soul,* Dan Allender and Tremper Longman—a psychologist and a theologian together writing about how our emotions reveal our deepest questions about God—tell us that "emotion links our internal and external worlds. To be aware of what we feel can open us to questions we would rather ignore. For many of us, that is precisely why it is easier not to feel."[4]

"The reason we don't want to feel is that feeling exposes the tragedy of our world and the darkness of our hearts."[5]

"One explanation for why we avoid our feelings is that it's painful to feel. To feel hurt, hurts. To feel shame, shames. To feel any loss only intensifies sorrow. . . . Perhaps a better explanation for why it's so difficult to feel our feelings is that all emotion, positive or negative, opens the door to the nature of reality. All of us prefer to avoid pain—but even more, we want to escape reality."[6]

Painful memories keep wounded emotions raw, because they reopen the hurt and bring all the feelings back. Some can have vivid memories of highly painful experiences, but their emotions have frozen at the surface. Nevertheless, their feelings and emotions still hide beneath the surface. We could compare them to a person trying to hold a bunch of balloons under water. He or she succeeds for a while, but over the course of a lifetime the memories below the surface pop up here and there despite a person's desperate efforts to bury them. Such repressed memories cannot be forgotten.

The harder we try to keep bad memories out of conscious recall, the more powerful they become. Since they are not allowed to enter directly through the door of our minds, they creep into our personalities in disguised and destructive ways—as guilt, depression, anger, fear, shame, despair—and a host of dysfunctional behaviors: hatred and resentment, alcoholism, obsessions, eating disorders, multiple marriages, or unhealthy attitudes toward sex.

How We're Doing With God

Allender and Longman take us to the heart of what the memory-forgetting moment in Joseph's life was all about. "What are we to listen for in our emotions? The answer is, in part: *We are to listen for the direction of our heart.* The question, *What do I feel?* is in fact another way of asking, *Who am I? What direction am I moving in?*

"We most often think of emotions in horizontal terms—how we're doing in relation to people in our lives. But in a deeper sense, emotions reveal what's happening on a vertical level. They provide a window on the question, *What am I doing with God?*

"The heart's movement can be calibrated and assessed in light of many different criteria, but all evaluations eventually boil down to this: *Am I moving toward God or away from Him?* Am I turning toward

God with awe and gratitude, or away from Him toward false gods of my own making?"[7]

While in academy and college I was on a gymnastic team. My specialty was the high bar. The high bar is that flexible single shaft supported on each end by posts nine feet or so above the mat. High-bar routines demand precision timing and an iron grip. The centrifugal force of a giant swing alone—a movement in which the hands grip the bar as the fully extended body swings a full 360-degree circle around the bar—can literally hurtle you across the gym with tremendous speed and a painful crash if your grip isn't strong enough. I know! It happened often during my first weeks of training. And it hurts. In time, though, I developed that iron grip.

We used a lot of chalk on the high bar. Chalk enhances grip, but it can also peel the skin right off your hand. Now, *that* hurts! If you don't have enough chalk, your hands can actually get slimy and you slip off easily. But if you use too much chalk, your hands will be so dry that they will literally squeak with every revolution. It is then that skin begins to peel. Any calluses on your hand are especially vulnerable to friction and need to be kept soft with oil or shaved smooth. They're the first to go when the chalk makes your grip squeak.

One thing became very clear to me early on. I had to take care of my hands. Because if I had any open wounds, if I tore the skin off the palms of my hands, no matter how firm my grip was, I just could not hold on. Just think with me now. You can say, "It's all in the head." Well, it *is* all in the head. And yet—it's not. The moment my wounded hand would grasp around the bar, I would feel incredible pain that would keep me from holding on. The pain from the open wounds in my palms would prevent me from keeping my grip even when I had the muscular strength to do so. No matter how strong my grip had become, the pain somehow seemed stronger. It stopped me from doing something I otherwise could do.

That is exactly what happens to many Christians with unhealed emotional scars. The very process of trying to believe in God's promises and of reaching out to take hold of His hand, or of letting go of certain memories about things in our lives, is too painful to bear. Reaching out for healing exerts great pressure on an emotional wound that we simply cannot cope with. So rather than deal with it, we let go. The questions and doubts that seem to be coming from our *heads* are actually arising out of deep buried hurts in our *hearts*. Something has so deeply damaged and distorted our concepts/feelings about God that we yield to doubt so we will not have to reopen those painful wounds.[8] Both reaching out to God and holding on to Him can be painful.

Joseph, though, chose to approach God. In the midst of one painful, humiliating, and crushing experience after another, he turned to His creator. The process of holding on to God caused pain so searing that he wanted to let go—but he nevertheless chose to cling to Him. Then, after Joseph had pursued a life of faithfulness to God no matter how he felt, God wonderfully removed the pain from those wounds.

In his book on Joseph, Gene Getz asks the burning question "What, then, did God enable Joseph to forget? It was the *pain* associated with those events. The emotional sting was gone. He was not in bondage to past experiences. There was no lingering bitterness, no inhibiting fear, no debilitating emotional sensitivity, and no obsessive thoughts, or compulsive behavior. Joseph had no regrets. God had healed his emotional memories."[9]

Such forgetting, as *The Interpreter's Bible* states "is not in the sense of their being wiped out of thought or canceled from experience, but rather in the sense that what had been bitter in them was transcended."[10] Neither Joseph nor God could do it alone. God could remove only the pain if Joseph, with his wounded hands, was willing to reach out in faith and hold on to Him and be real about what was going on in his life and how he felt about it.

When we read this passage, we get the sense that Joseph was conscious of what God was performing in his life. And when Asenath bore Joseph a second son, Joseph chose another name that focused on what God was accomplishing—Ephraim, " 'for,' he said, 'God has made me fruitful in the land of my affliction' " (Gen. 41:52). Joseph had not forgotten what he suffered in Egypt. But he was now rejoicing in what God was doing in his life—removing the pain from agonizing memories and creating fruitfulness amid affliction. The trials only made him more appreciative of God's present blessing and emotional healing in his life. Joseph chose not to dwell on his painful memories, but on the God who was with him when those events happened. No matter how raw his emotions, how painful his feelings, his inner world always turned toward God.

At this point in the story, of course, Joseph had no way of knowing that he would ever meet his brothers again, and that when he would encounter them it would reopen a host of feelings that through God's help he would be able to lay aside. We will soon come to those dramatic moments of reunion. For now, though, all that Joseph knew was that God had given him a new life in Egypt and had allowed him to move beyond the pain he had felt in the past.

While studying for this chapter I ran across an absolutely incredible promise in Psalm 84:5-7. In my opinion, several of the paraphrased versions of the Bible pick up the heart of the passage's meaning better than the study versions. This is especially so in verse 6, where the psalm refers to the Valley of Baca, or the Baca Valley. The term *baca* means "weeping." It comes from the Hebrew word for weep, which is *bakah*. In fact, *bakah* is the word used in this story wherever Joseph wept (Gen. 42:24; 43:30; 45:2, 14). Because Baca means weeping, some translate verse 6 of this psalm as referring to the Valley of Weeping. It fits the overall point. Listen to the absolutely incredible beauty of this verse:

"How happy are those who find their source of strength in you and who travel the road to Zion! When they pass through the Valley of Weeping, they will find a spring of comfort. Blessings will fall on them like a gentle rain. They will go on from strength to strength until they see you face to face" (Ps. 84:5-7, Clear Word).

In the midst of the Valley of Weeping, no matter what we are enduring, God has promised to be there and let His blessings, like gentle rain, shower down upon us. Isn't that exciting? We can go on through the valley of weeping from strength to strength until we meet God face-to-face. Isn't that incredible?

Hurt, humiliation, horror, and hate fill so many of our memories. Like Joseph we bleed inside, and our very soul cries out for healing. Some of our memories seep out in dysfunctional behaviors and interpersonal conflicts. But Genesis proclaims the good news that God wants to bring the same kind of healing to your soul as He gave Joseph. He longs to remove the pain from your bad memories.

And He desires to make you fruitful in the very place of your afflic-tion. Drawing you to Himself, He will surround you with His lov-ing arms of grace and healing.

"Emotions are the language of the soul. They are the cry that gives the heart a voice."[11] It is important to listen to our emotions, to what is going on deep down inside us. Painful memories and the emotions and feelings they stir in our hearts reveal how we're doing with God and what direction we are going in. "Are you pursuing God?—your emotions will tell you. Are you pursuing false gods?—your emotional life will provide strong clues to the nature of your soul's direction."[12]

Jesus calls us to Himself with the incredible words, "Come to me, all of you who are tired from carrying heavy loads, and I will give you rest" (Matt. 11:28, TEV).

He does not promise a quick-fix solution, however, or answers that will alleviate the struggle. Instead, we encounter a Person—one who says, "I am there. I am with you." The One we find is a living God who cares for us with all His heart. And when with our wounded hands we reach out and cling to Him—no matter how painful that grasp might be—there and there alone is the promise of healing.

---

[1] W. M. Taylor, *Joseph the Prime Minister*, p. 94.

[2] V. E. Frankl, *Man's Search for Meaning*, p. 58.

[3] David A. Seamands, *Healing of Memories* (Wheaton, Ill.: Victor Brooks, 1985), p. 15.

[4] Dan B. Allender and Tremper Longman III, *The Cry of the Soul: How Our Emotions Reveal Our Deepest Questions About God* (Colorado Springs, Colo.: NavPress, 1994), p. 20.

[5] *Ibid.*, p. 14.

[6] *Ibid.*, p. 21.

[7] *Ibid.*, p. 25.

[8] Seamands, p. 114.

[9] G. A. Getz, *Joseph*, p. 121.

[10] *The Interpreter's Bible* (Nashville: Abingdon, 1972), vol. 1, pp. 780, 781.

[11] Allender and Longman, p. 25.

[12] *Ibid.*, p. 16.

CHAPTER 11

Flashbacks, Panic Attacks, and Tough Love

GENESIS 42:1-17

One of Vladimir Nabokov's famous short stories tells of Ostend, a biology professor who received word from a private detective he had hired that his wife back in London was unfaithful to him. An intercepted letter, written in her minuscule, familiar handwriting, began, "My dear darling Jack, I am still all full of your last kiss." The professor's name was certainly not Jack—that was the whole point. The idea of her unfaithfulness filled him with a sharp and cold hatred. He realized then and there that he would get even by murdering her. Feeling no qualms, he decided that he only had to devise the most excruciating, most ingenious method possible.

Now, his wife had actually been dabbling with the spirit world. A medium occasionally visited her at home. Ostend's wife told of seeing ghosts in the house. Odd things would happen to her, such as the dream she had about a dead youth with whom, before her marriage, she had strolled in the twilight and kissed. The next morning, still absorbed with his image, she had penciled a letter to him—a letter to her dream. She had simply wanted to send a little warmth to the spectral visitor, to reassure him with some words from earth. The letter vanished mysteriously from her writing pad, and the same night she dreamed of a long table, from under which Jack suddenly emerged, nodding to her gratefully. Now, for some reason, she felt uneasy when recalling that dream, almost as if she had cheated on her husband with a ghost. After all, she really did love the eccentric old professor.

The biology professor had warned his wife many times that she was playing with fire in her dabbling with the supernatural, but she just brushed him off as too intellectual and old-fashioned. On this particular trip abroad he had acquired a rare skeleton of a hunchback for the museum of the university he worked at. He brought it back in a large orange suitcase and took it home with him the night he arrived back in London.

Sitting around supper that night, he asked, "Well, did your ghosts come knocking while I was away? You know something," he went on, sprinkling some sugar on some pink rhubarb, "you and your friends are playing with fire. There can be terrifying occurrences." Then he went on to share a frightening story that a Viennese doctor had told him about a Hungarian fortuneteller who suddenly became hysterical and died of a heart attack. When he arrived at her candlelit hut and undressed her, the doctor was stunned by the sight of her body. As the doctor watched, her corpse slowly began to unwind like a huge ball of yarn. Her body, like a thin endless worm, disentangled itself and slithered out through the crack under the door. All that remained on the bed was a naked, white, still-moist skeleton. "Yet this woman had a husband," he added, who had once "kissed that worm."

By now his wife was visibly shaken. Her pale shoulders gave a shiver. "You don't realize what a terrifying thing you've told me," she said in agitation. "So the woman's ghost disappeared into a worm? It's all terrifying . . ."

The professor faked a yawn, tapping his clenched fist against his lips. "I'm tired. I'm going to bed now. Please don't turn on the light when you come in. Get right into bed with me—with me," he repeated meaningfully and tenderly, as he had not spoken for a long time. And off he went.

When she came to bed later that night she dutifully left the light off. But in the darkness it seemed that all the objects in the room were watching her expectantly. A wind of fear chilled her. She reached out her arm to locate the headboard of the bed, then lay down on its edge. She knew she was not alone, that her husband was lying beside her. For a few moments she motionlessly gazed up into the darkness, feeling the fierce, muffled pounding of her heart.

When her eyes had become accustomed to the dark, she turned

her head toward her husband. He was lying with his back toward her, wrapped in a blanket. All she could see was the bald crown of his head which seemed extraordinarily sleek and white in a puddle of moonlight. *He's not asleep,* she thought affectionately. *If he were, he would be snoring a little.* Smiling, she slid over toward her husband, spreading her arms under the covers for the familiar embrace. Her fingers felt some smooth ribs. Her knee struck a smooth bone. A skull rolled from the pillow onto her shoulder. When the professor turned on the light and emerged from behind the screen, the blanket and sheets, jumbled together, slithered to the floor. His wife lay dead of a heart attack, embracing the white, hastily cobbled skeleton of the hunchback.[1]

If anyone ever had the opportunity to retaliate and get even with a vengeance, it was Joseph. And if anyone ever had the resources to devise the most excruciating, most ingenious method to exact revenge, it was also he. By this point in the story Joseph was Egypt's prime minister with absolute power at his disposal. He literally held people's destiny in his hands. Jacob's words to his sons unwittingly foreshadow the extent of Joseph's power: "Behold, I have heard that there is grain in Egypt; go down there and buy some for us from that place, so that we may live and not die" (Gen. 42:2). Life or death— Joseph held the key.[2]

Now his brothers arrive, and we find Joseph acting in some most unexpected ways, given all that we have seen in his character to date. Now Joseph appears impatient, rough, capricious, coldhearted, and merciless. He speaks harshly (verse 7), throws his brothers in prison (verse 17), and threatens to kill the whole lot of them (verse 20). Then he jerks them around by hiding their money in their bags (verse 25). When they return for more grain, Joseph treats them to a lavish banquet only to throw them off balance some more by having his silver cup planted in Benjamin's bag, accusing them of thievery, and declaring that Benjamin will become his slave (Gen. 43:16–44:34).

The whole strategy Joseph follows is both ingenious and excruciating. It leaves every one of his brothers thoroughly shaken and terrified. Stripped of every rag of self-confidence or hope, they fear they will be executed or enslaved. Is God finally exacting justice for their long-held secret crime? It's a wonder that none of them had a heart attack, especially Judah when he realized that Benjamin was in big trouble (Gen. 44:14-34; 43:8, 9).

Our first reaction is that Joseph's hot under the collar and putting on the squeeze. That he is up to a slow and calculating revenge. Genesis clearly tells us that Joseph was testing his brothers. But why? Did he get some sadistic enjoyment out of it? Was he waiting to forgive if they could prove they had really changed or were sorry? Or was he holding out until the very last minute before giving in? What motivated Joseph? Was it revenge? Could he be trying to get even with his brothers for what they had done to him? Or was the whole process something he needed in order to work through things in his own heart?

Joseph certainly faced the temptation to retaliate. His brothers had treated him cruelly, and he had endured a long list of painful experiences. Imagine for a moment what he must have felt when he looked up and saw 10 men bowing low before him. As usual he stood at his post, surrounded by all the confusion and noise of an Eastern bazaar, when all of a sudden the sight of 10 familiar faces caught his attention. Immediately recognizing his brothers, Joseph no doubt found himself confronted with old wounds and a host of feelings he had so nicely tucked away by God's grace. All those painful memories of his trials and his family that God had caused him to forget now suddenly rushed into his consciousness once more. Sometimes we can bring ourselves to forgive—theoretically, at least—when persons are absent, but when we encounter them face-to-face it unleashes all kinds of emotions and feelings. When we see them coming into the church foyer or walking toward us on the sidewalk, suddenly we have a hard time facing those very same people we thought we had forgiven. Forgiveness suddenly is more difficult and personal.

Corrie ten Boom spoke in a church in Munich on how God forgives—freely, completely. It was an incredible message the people in defeated Germany needed to hear. A sea of solemn faces stared back at her, not quite daring to believe that God was so merciful, so gracious, so compassionate. Then she spotted him working his way toward her through the crowd. One moment she saw the overcoat and the brown hat he was carrying, the next a blue uniform and a visored cap with its skull and crossbones. It came back with a rush: the huge room with its pile of dresses and shoes in the center of the floor; the shame of walking naked past this man; her sister Betsie's frail form ahead of her, ribs sharp beneath the parchment skin. The man approaching her had been one of the most cruel guards at the Nazi concentration camp where Betsie had died.

Now he stood in front of her, hand thrust out. "A fine message, Fraulein! How good it is to know that, as you say, all our sins are at the bottom of the sea!"

Corrie was face-to-face again with one of her captors, and her blood seemed to freeze. She had spoken so glibly of forgiveness, grace, and compassion. Suddenly she confronted the reality that although she could talk of forgiveness day and night, she herself had to forgive—not in the abstract, not some person whose image had blurred with time, but a real person who had hurt her deeply. Her arm was like lead, and she couldn't lift it to take his in greeting. She stood there—one whose sins had again and again been forgiven— unable to forgive. Betsie had died in that place. Could he erase her slow, terrible death simply for the asking? It was the most difficult moment in her life. Coldness clutched at her heart. "Jesus, help me!" she silently prayed. "I can lift my hand. I can do that much. You supply the feeling."[3]

"The temptation to vindicate ourselves or to retaliate is normal," Gene Getz explains, "especially when we meet face to face with those who have offended and hurt us. At that moment, whether or not we have *truly* forgiven is put to the test. It's easier to *forget* the pain and hurt when we're separated physically. But when we interface, all the old mental and emotional memories tend to come to the surface."[4]

That's where Joseph finds himself—put to the test in that incredible dramatic moment.

Genesis immediately pushes aside any notion, any possibility, of retaliation or revenge, though, with the statement that "Joseph remembered the dreams which he dreamed about them" (Gen. 42:9). As Joseph watched his brothers bowing down before him, he had flashbacks to those dreams he had had as a teenage boy. In a moment like that the mind does strange things. His emotions had already been churning, but now his mind began to work. When Joseph saw his brothers bowing down to him emotion must have overwhelmed him. His dreams had literally come true. What happened at that moment became a master key in unlocking his understanding of why God had allowed him to be sold into Egypt. "You meant evil against me, but God meant it for good" (Gen. 50:20). Here we have a clue that Joseph's schemes and plans against his brothers had as their motivation his earlier dreams and not revenge for what his brothers had done to him. God had already brought unusual healing to Joseph's heart from the painful memories. Since he had already forgiven his brothers, he was prepared for this dramatic moment.

If you have any question about Joseph's motives, you need to catch the "curious contrast" in Joseph's behavior.[5] "And he turned away from them and wept. But when he returned to them and spoke to them, he took Simeon from them and bound him before their eyes" (Gen. 42:24). He turns away to cry, then returns to tie Simeon up in front of them. Joseph's brothers saw only the latter of the two actions and must have thought him rough and unkind. They must have trembled in his presence. But they didn't know the heart of love beating beneath the seeming hardness. Nor could they ever in their wildest imagination guess that Joseph kept Simeon as "a silken cord" to bring them back to him again or as part of the process of awakening the memory of another brother whom they had lost years before.[6] If Joseph had let them all go without keeping Simeon, he might never have seen them again.

Sometimes it's like that with God. William Cowper catches that reality in his familiar hymn, "God Moves in a Mysterious Way":

> "Judge not the Lord by feeble sense,
> But trust Him for His grace;
> Behind a frowning providence,
> He hides a smiling face."[7]

Often things come to us in life that make us think God frowns on us. When life gets tough, and we suffer, endure imprisonment, bereavement, or rebuke, we regard God as harsh and hard. We feel that He is against us. But He's not. A heart of love beats behind it all. "We little realize how much pain He is suffering as He causes us pain or how the tender heart of our brother is filled with grief, welling up within Him as He makes Himself strange and deals so roughly with us."[8]

Awakening Conscience

What was Joseph up to, if it wasn't retaliation or slow revenge? He now knew that in God's providence he must bring only good and blessing to his family. But first Joseph needed some questions answered. Was his father still alive? And what about Benjamin? He counted only 10 there in front of him. Benjamin was missing. Had they killed him, too? Were they sorry for what they had done to him? Had they changed? Where was God in their lives by now? If he had revealed himself immediately, some things he might never have learned. Consequently Joseph chose to use a strategy that must have created intense pain for him personally.[9] Forcing himself to control his emotions, he acted as if he didn't know them, and in the process came across harsh and indifferent. If you read the story carefully, everything they had done to him he now did to them, but with a different motive. He wanted to know what was going on in their hearts and what had happened since he had seen them last.

Through the process of Joseph's probing, something deeper began to take place in his brother's hearts—they came face-to-face with the skeletons in their closet. At the end of their three days in prison, Joseph said, "Do this and live, for I fear God: if you are honest men, let one of your brothers be confined in your prison; but as for the rest of you, go, carry grain for the famine of your households, and bring your youngest brother to me, so your words may be verified, and you will not die" (Gen. 42:18-20).

Joseph was out to get the facts, dealing with the issue that "you guys say you are honest men, but you may not be as honest as you think."

His brothers nervously said one to another, "Truly we are guilty concerning our brother, because we saw the distress of his soul when he pleaded with us, yet we would not listen; therefore this distress has come upon us." And Reuben answered them saying, "Did I not tell you, 'Do not sin against the boy'; and you would not listen? Now comes the reckoning for his blood" (verses 21, 22).

They spoke in front of Joseph, not realizing that he knew Hebrew. What's going on here? It's a very simple thing. Guilt has a way of coming to the surface when the going becomes tough. When life runs smoothly we can easily forget the things we've done in the past to people, the sins in our lives. But when life starts getting filled with hard knocks, when suddenly we begin getting squeezed from unexpected directions, conscience deep down begins to ask itself, "I wonder if there's something I've done. Something God's punishing me for." For more than 20 years Joseph's brothers had tried to hide their sin. They had buried their horrible crime. Probably they had even refused to talk about it at all until this very moment. Suddenly they felt themselves under conviction over what they had done to Joseph. As they prepared to leave, they discussed it openly with one another—probably acknowledging their sin for the first time in those 20 years. Their conscience was awakening.

Joseph's strategy succeeded. And through it all, God was the one working. The Lord used the severe famine to bring the sons of Jacob face-to-face with their brother Joseph (Gen. 42:5-8). And when they encountered Joseph, they would come face-to-face with their own hearts, their own private inner world of conscience (verses 21, 22). The memory of what they did to Joseph began to gnaw at their conscience. Later, when they found the money in their sacks, they turned trembling to one another, asking, "What is this that God has done to us?" (verse 28).

Their words have an ironic ring to them, pointing us to the work of God. As the story unfolds, it seems as if everywhere they turned they heard the echo of their mistreatment of Joseph. Now, they had declared themselves "honest men" (verses 11, 19), but they really weren't, because they were hiding an incredible skeleton in their closet. When accused of stealing Joseph's cup, they said, "Why does my lord speak such words as these? Far be it from your servants to do such a thing" (Gen. 44:7). "We would never steal your cup. We would never do anything like that." But the fact was, they had done something more terrible. In the end—by the time you trace the story of Joseph's meeting his brothers to the moment when he reveals himself to them—they stand stripped of every rag of self-confidence and are totally at Joseph's mercy. It says something about the gospel—how every one of us must finally be stripped of absolutely all self-confidence and be entirely in the hands of redeeming grace.

"When Judah and his brothers came to Joseph's house, he was still there, and they fell to the ground before him. And Joseph said to them, 'What is this deed that you have done? Do you not know that such a man as I can indeed practice divination?'" (verses 14, 15).

Joseph was saying, "Don't you know I can read people's hearts? I know what you're really like." Now, Joseph was faking it here, but they would have never guessed it. "So Judah said, 'What can we say to my Lord? What can we speak? And how can we justify ourselves? God has found out the iniquity of your servants'" (verse 16).

Notice that they hadn't stolen that silver cup. They weren't admitting to that guilt. They were responding to something deeper. "How can we justify ourselves? God has found out our iniquity!" Their words take on the form of a confession. While it had first looked as if he was working a slow revenge upon his brothers, we can see that his goal was not revenge but repentance. His brothers had a host of things in their past that they needed to deal with. They had forgotten, and hence unforgiven, sins. Forgotten or hidden sins are also unforgiven (Prov. 28:13). It is only the acknowledged, confessed sin that God can forgive and cleanse us from (1 John 1:8-2:2). He cannot free us from something that we refuse to accept that we even have. Joseph's ploy led his brothers to an awareness of their guilt, and they were now, for the first time, ready to acknowledge that guilt.[10]

It is a story of God graciously awakening the men's consciences from their long sleep.[11] As Meyer yearns: "Well would it be if some resurrection trumpet could sound and awaken the sleeping consciences of men, causing long forgotten but unforgiven sins to arise and come forth from their graves. Of what use is it to present the Savior to those who do not feel they need Him?"[12]

The Way of Grace

We have here, then, a story of incredible grace! The brothers did not realize that Joseph and God had already forgiven them. Before that wonderful truth could dawn on them, however, God's grace led them down a path that crushed their hearts until they had absolutely no place to go but to confess and fall upon the mercy of the one who had found them out. We must sense our need for forgiveness and repent before we can experience the joy of grace and forgiveness.

In his classic book on Joseph, Meyer points to the heart of God's gracious work to save: "The great Physician never heals over a wound from above but heals from below, and only after careful probing and searching. The foundations of noble character must touch the rock of genuine repentance."[13]

In other words, God doesn't heal from the top. He doesn't just put a bandage over our spiritual and moral wounds and then set us on our way. As the healing of a wound occurs from within, so God does His work of cleansing, renewing, empowering, and healing deep down in our inner private world. That's what God was at work doing with Joseph's brothers. Reaching right into the very depths of their hearts, He pricked, then healed.

A. A. Proctor writes:

> "Kind hearts are here; yet would the tenderest one
> Have limits to its mercy: God has none.
> And man's forgiveness may be true and sweet,
> But yet he stoops to give it. More complete
> Is Love that lays forgiveness at thy feet,
> And pleads with thee to raise it. Only heaven
> Means crowned, not vanquished, when it says 'Forgiven!'"[14]

Read it again, more carefully. "More complete is love that lays forgiveness at the feet, and pleads with thee to raise it." Complete love is the love that lays forgiveness at our feet—does everything to open up our need for that forgiveness—and then places it before us and begs us to accept it. That is God's love, His awakening grace.

Jacob's farewell words to his sons provide the narrative key to what follows: "May God Almighty grant you mercy before the man" (Gen 43:14, NIV). When Joseph finally reveals himself to his brothers, Scripture tells us that "he was deeply stirred over his brother" (verse 30, NASB). It is important for us to see how, in Jacob's words, the compassion that Joseph found toward his brothers came from "God Almighty." God was at work both in Joseph and through Joseph. The same God works for you as He yearns for your heart, lays forgiveness at your feet, and begs you to pick it up. Take it into your heart and find peace, assurance, and renewal.

And so we find here an incredible expression of grace. But it is not cheap grace! Cheap grace comes to us without the surrender of our heart. Joseph realized that he could not just forgive his brothers. If he had revealed himself at the beginning, declaring, "I forgive you. Let's get on with our life. God meant it all for good!" his brothers would never have really dealt with their past or what was going on in their lives. Joseph refused to enter the pit of cheap grace. The only way for complete and total reconciliation with him or God was for them to experience what only God could do in their lives—resurrect conscience, make them aware of their need for grace, and then apply that grace to them from within. He must lay forgiveness at their feet and beg them to pick it up.

By refusing cheap grace and through his harshness, through the rough way he led them, amid the excruciating pain of an enlivened conscience, Joseph revealed God's true grace. Grace-filled love constantly devises means of expressing itself. So Joseph put money in their sacks, invited them into his home, and treated them to a feast. He instructed his stewards to treat his brothers kindly, and then wished them God's grace. Here we find a marvelous picture of God's incredible grace as He churns up our hearts and does not let us go until we have faced any sin that we have forgotten and left unforgiven. He blesses us as at the same time He leads us to face who we really are.

The Bible tells us unequivocally, "If we confess our sins, he is faithful and just to forgive us our sins, and to cleanse us from all unrighteousness" (1 John 1:9, KJV). Joseph helped lead his brothers to the moment when they would confess their sins. If there is anything in your life that you have left forgotten and thus unforgiven, let God's Spirit open your heart, your mind. Let it happen! For it is in that experience alone that God can apply grace. Then you can rejoice in the free gift of salvation that only Jesus Christ can give you.

---

[1] Vladimir Nabokov, "Revenge," *The Stories of Vladimir Nabokov* (New York: Alfred A. Knopf, 1995), pp. 67-73.

[2] J. H. Sailhamer, *The Pentateuch as Narrative,* p. 216.

[3] Corrie ten Boom, *Tramp for the Lord* (Old Tappan, N.J.: Fleming H. Revell Co., 1974), pp. 55-57.

[4] G. A. Getz, *Joseph,* p. 132.

[5] F. B. Meyer, *The Life of Joseph,* p. 69.

[6] *Ibid.*

[7] William Cowper, "God Moves in a Mysterious Way," *The Seventh-day Adventist Hymnal* (Hagerstown, Md.: Review and Herald Pub. Assn., 1985), No. 107.

[8] Meyer, p. 69.

[9] Getz, p. 137.

[10] Sailhamer, p. 221.

[11] Meyer, pp. 63, 64.

[12] *Ibid.,* p. 64.

[13] *Ibid.,* p. 63.

[14] *Ibid.,* p. 71.

CHAPTER 12

The Sound of A Man Forgiving— Breaking the Cycle of Ungrace

GENESIS 45:1-5

Ever since his brothers' appearance in Egypt Joseph had struggled to keep a cap on his feelings and maintain control over events. Up to this point he had revealed little emotion to his brothers. As far as they were concerned, he was a stern, coldhearted Egyptian ruler who had a way of jerking people around. But when Judah reached the end of his last-ditch appeal for mercy—the very brother who had once suggested selling Joseph into slavery actually pleading that he be allowed to take Benjamin's place as a slave—Joseph could no longer constrain himself. The powerful urge to reveal his identity now overwhelmed him. Unwittingly Judah had pushed Joseph's emotional "hot buttons," invoking images of his father, his dead mother, and his youngest brother. What makes the scene so dramatic is that while Judah is consciously trying to evoke Joseph's pity, he has no idea that he is actually addressing his long-lost brother for whom his words have unbearable associations (Gen. 44:18-34).[1] Judah's confession had unraveled his soul and satisfied Joseph that his brothers were sorry. They had changed.

"Then Joseph could not control himself before all those who stood by him, and he cried, 'Have everyone go out from me.' So there was no man with him when Joseph made himself known to his brothers. And he wept so loudly that the Egyptians heard it" (Gen. 45:1, 2).

In this climactic scene the sound of Joseph's wailing voice literally echoes throughout the palace. We can only imagine what his brothers must have thought or felt when they saw their accuser begin to lose emotional control and then heard him turn to his attendants and announce, "I want everyone out of here. Now!"

At this moment Joseph's brothers were on trial. Benjamin had been accused of stealing Joseph's silver cup and Judah had pleaded for mercy. The whole lot of them were writhing in agony and fear. Guilt blasted through their awakened conscience like a hurricane. Powerless and vulnerable, they had rent their clothes in grief. When they saw everyone leave the room and heard Joseph's outburst, they could only conclude that the ax was about to fall. Would it be death or slavery? In absolutely no way could they have interpreted Joseph's reactions as positive. They must have recoiled from his emotional outburst with intense fear.[2] Even as his Egyptian attendants no doubt listened to the unusual sounds coming from behind those closed doors, they too could not help wondering what they heard. Was it joy? grief? a fit of anger?

Some have suggested it was "pent-up emotion." They tell us that Joseph had been in agonizing suspense from the moment he recognized his brothers and began to play out his ingenious and excruciating test. Afraid that they might not pass the test, he was anxious not to lose them again. Now that the tension was removed, all he could do was wail.[3] Without doubt, Joseph did experience deep emotional release!

A few times in my life I have witnessed a man or a woman break down uncontrollably and sob so loudly that if I had stepped out of the room or even house I could still have heard them. People usually experience this kind of deep emotional sobbing at either of two times during their lives. "Either we are feeling deep sorrow and emotional pain or we're experiencing psychological release."[4] I've seen it happen when a person has lost a loved one or when a son shows up at the bedside of a father who has just died without the opportunity to make things right with his parent. And I've seen such a reaction when someone has watched a spouse walk out the door and file for divorce. So there's either deep sorrow and emotional pain, or we're experiencing some psychological release. One of those famous photographs taken of the liberation of Paris forever captured the weeping face of a well-dressed Frenchman. The tension of the Nazi occupation and the Allied invasion was indescribable. When freedom finally came it was such an incredible release that all he could do was publically weep.

117

While undoubtedly Joseph went through a deep emotional release, I think Yancey comes closest to the point: "It was the sound of a man forgiving. Behind every act of forgiveness lies a wound of betrayal."[5] "The sound of a man forgiving." Forgiveness is a painful experience and not easy to do. We do not forgive casually, nor do we receive it without great emotion. All forgiveness is achingly difficult. So is reconciliation. Closure on broken relationships and old wounds is an extremely painful experience! Once we get through that trauma we're excited—excited that closure has come, that reconciliation has taken place. But the process is an excruciating and often messy experience. As Elizabeth O'Connor writes: "Despite a hundred sermons on forgiveness, we do not forgive easily, nor find ourselves easily forgiven. Forgiveness, we discover, is always harder than the sermons make it out to be."[6] In his book *What's So Amazing About Grace,* Yancey calls forgiveness "an unnatural act."[7]

If forgiveness is always painful, what does it sound like to forgive? Hear the wail of Joseph's grief and his love echoing throughout the palace. It reverberates everywhere. That's the sound of someone forgiving.

Lewis Smedes tells us that forgiveness is a personal drama with at least five scenes and cannot be complete until each one plays itself out. The first scene involves holding the person who hurt us responsible and accountable. None of us likes conflict. It's easier to sometimes just let things slide. To forget about it, to make excuses, or to tell ourselves that it doesn't matter. Many are afraid to forgive, thinking that if they do, in some way or another they will be either condoning that person's behavior or that it will be letting the individual off the hook. But we will forgive them only if we hold them responsible for what they did to us.

The second scene occurs when we surrender our right to get even, our right to fairness. We agree to live with an untied score. Scene three revises our caricature of the person who hurt us. All of us have pretty good imaginations and graphic ways of depicting those who wound us. From within our pain we call names, infer motives, attach labels. Perhaps we depict them as monsters. But the process of forgiveness means that we must change our monster back into the weak and faulty human being she or he really is. Then we revise our feelings for that person in scene four. When we come to the place where compassion and sorrow replace anger and hatred we will be able to focus on what's best for the other person's needs and welfare. Finally, we accept the person who made us feel unacceptable.[8] None of these steps is easy. Nor are they painless. They are, however, indescribably freeing.

During his years in Egypt Joseph had gone through this forgiving flow. Now he faced his brothers. We have already learned how it is one thing to forgive someone when they are out of our view, blurred somewhat in our imagination by the passing of time. It's quite another thing altogether to extend that forgiveness when we meet them face-to-face. When they show up out of nowhere (or by appointment), what we've done in our heart we now need to express openly.

Grace Sounds the Best

Initially Joseph's brothers could not have interpreted his reactions as positive. No way would they have known that the wail they heard was the sound of a man forgiving and taking them one step closer to reconciliation. They must have recoiled from Joseph's emotional outburst with intense fear. And when he revealed his identity, they were undoubtedly numb. Scripture tells us that "his brothers could not answer him, for they were dismayed at his presence" (Gen. 45:3). *Patriarchs and Prophets* adds that "his brothers stood motionless, dumb with fear and amazement. . . . All their ill treatment of him passed before them."[9]

Predictably, their fear and anxiety suddenly turned to distress and self-hatred. Shame consumed them. How could they look into Joseph's eyes? How could they have been so evil? At that moment their feelings of remorse, regret, and guilt must have been absolutely overwhelming.

Clearly Joseph held all the cards and could play them exactly as he wished, and they knew it! There he stood, second to none but Pharaoh in all the land of Egypt. Legions of warriors, like those depicted on the Egyptian architecture around them, waited at his beck and call. Now that they were completely in his power, they just knew he would avenge the wrong that he had suffered.[10]

While his stunned brothers struggled to believe what they were hearing—wondering what might come next—Joseph's true character shone through. No doubt when he began to wail, they took a fearful step backward. When he revealed his true identity, they likely retreated still more. But Joseph invited them to approach him and put them at ease with gentle words that restored their dignity. "Then Joseph said to his brothers, 'Please come closer to me.' And they came closer. And he said, 'I am your brother Joseph, whom you sold into Egypt. And now do not be grieved or angry with yourselves, because you sold me here; for God sent me before you to preserve life. . . . God sent me before you to preserve for you a remnant in the earth, and to keep you alive by a great deliverance'" (verses 4-7).

Joseph's actions and words are magnanimous and extremely sensitive and designed to help his brothers at an embarrassingly awkward moment. They expected ungrace, but Joseph treated them graciously. Giving them what they didn't expect—grace—he pointed them to God and wanted them to see that the Lord had an ultimate purpose in all that had happened. Joseph desired for them to look past their failures and mistakes to God's gracious work. He sought to show them that both God and he cared for them. Their brother promised to provide for their personal needs (verse 11).

In his book *Shame and Grace* Lewis Smedes has a chapter he entitled "Singing 'Amazing Grace' Without Feeling Like a Wretch." You know the song: "Amazing grace! how sweet the sound, that saved a wretch like me!" Well, Smedes asks an interesting question: "How does grace make us feel?" "Now, I may be a wretch that grace has saved, but now that I am saved, do I still feel like a wretch?" Good question. So, Smedes suggests, when grace comes to us graciously, it heals. But when someone offers us grace ungraciously, it shames. You can tell that grace is gracious if it makes you feel better for having it—makes you feel like the worthy human being you are. While you may be a spiritual wretch, grace doesn't leave you feeling that way. "The question is: are we accepted by grace only in spite of our unworthiness or are we also accepted precisely because we are worthy? A grace that makes us feel worse for having it is an ungracious grace and therefore not really grace at all. If grace heals our shame, it must be a grace that tells us we are worthy to have it."[11] Now, that's an interesting twist!

"When we feel like wretches saved by grace we do not deserve," Smedes adds, "we may also discover a worth within that makes us worthy of the grace that saved us."[12] "Grace graciously given honors our worth as it overlooks our undeserving."[13] "Grace does not make me feel less; it makes me feel more worthy."[14] That's how God treats us. Marvelous, isn't it? How many times, though, have we forgiven someone but said, "Don't you ever do it again!" Or how many times have we felt that we have been bighearted, but the person we've been magnanimous to has gone away feeling really bad? They sense that they're living under our bighearted thumb, and it fills them with tremendous shame!

Joseph could easily have burst out with smug anger and exclaimed, "You guys sold me into slavery. But you know what? I'm above that kind of stuff. I'm going to forgive you." And then as time went on he could have just rubbed it in here and there, reminding them how big he was to forgive little people like them, in the process dragging out the shame. But he didn't. No, Joseph invited them to come closer. It's as if he's saying, "Look into my eyes. See beyond your sins and your shame to God and His gracious work. He has taken the fragmented pieces of our lives and created a wonderful mosaic of hope and mighty salvation." Egypt's prime minister chose to lead his brothers past himself to God.

The first thing the shamed prodigal son tried to tell his father was "Dad, I don't feel worthy to be called a son anymore. Take me on as a hired hand. I'll live in the barn." What did that father do? What does grace do? Grace took off the robe and put it on the son, embracing him. It removed the family ring and slipped it on the finger. Throwing a neighborhood party, grace received him back into the family as a beloved son. His dignity raised, he felt value and worth, not because of what he'd done or what he could do, but because his father loved him. Grace always ascribes worth and value to hurting people, and it is fueled by love.

After their father died, the brothers thought for sure Joseph would get even. That grace was just a cover. "When Joseph's brothers saw that their father was dead, they said, 'What if Joseph should bear a grudge against us and pay us back in full for all the wrong which we did to him!' So they sent a message to Joseph, saying,

'Your father charged before he died, saying, "Thus you shall say to Joseph, 'Please forgive, I beg you, the transgression of your brothers and their sin, for they did you wrong.' And now, please forgive the transgression of the servants of the God of your father. And Joseph wept when they spoke to him" (Gen. 50:15-17).

"But Joseph said to them, 'Do not be afraid, for am I in God's place? And as for you, you meant evil against me, but God meant it for good in order to bring about this present result, to preserve many people alive. So therefore, do not be afraid; I will provide for you and your little ones.' So he comforted them and spoke kindly to them" (verses 19-21).

Again Joseph comforted his brothers, speaking kindly to them and promising to take care of them. He reminded them of God's providence and ways. And he asked, "Am I in God's place?"

Yet how godlike Joseph's character was at that moment. Everything he did mirrored grace. Joseph stands out here as a model, a picture of God's character. All the things that Joseph had done had led his brothers to that heart-wrenching experience of awakening conscience. Then he extended this incredible grace by giving them a home and making them feel important. That's what God is like! Joseph was mirroring the divine character.

The most touching scene in our story appears in Genesis 45:15. It tells us that Joseph went from brother to brother (one by one) kissing them and exchanging words of reconciliation. Then "afterward his brothers talked with him." Do you remember how the story of Joseph began? There in Canaan his brothers "hated him and could not speak to him on friendly terms" (Gen. 37:4). The story begins with Joseph's brothers not being able to relate to him at all and ends up with some highly personal dialogue. At one point they could not say a peaceful word to Joseph. Now they can look him in the eyes and talk like brothers. Healing has taken place. While forgiveness is painful, and grace not our usual or natural way of relating to those who have hurt us, the process of forgiveness and grace leads to communication. The pain of forgiveness opens that door of communication. The way of grace establishes relationship. That's what God desires between ourselves and others. If we're husband and wife, siblings, members of a congregation, or anyone else not talking with each other, God wants that communication rebuilt. It's not going to be an easy process. But that is the goal, the direction grace leads—the restoration of communication and relationship. Here in Genesis we find a paradigm of reconciliation and redemption. It is the moment that God longs for with each one of us.

Breaking the Cycle of Ungrace

Philip Yancey tells the story of one family that spans a century of ungrace. It began with 100-year-old Daisy and the painful memories of her "mean drunk" father. Daisy used to cower in the corner, sobbing, as her drunken father kicked her baby brother and sister across the linoleum floor. She hated him with all her heart. One day her father declared that he wanted his wife out of the house by noon. That was it. She was gone never to return. Some of the children eventually rejoined their mother, and some went to live with other relatives. It was Daisy's lot, though, to stay with her father. She grew up with a hard knot of bitterness inside her, a tumor of hatred from what he had done to the family. In time Daisy's father vanished—no one knew where he had gone, and no one cared.

Many years later, to everyone's surprise, the father resurfaced. He had found the Lord and was a changed man. One by one he looked up his children to ask for forgiveness. He didn't defend anything that had happened—he couldn't make it right. But he was sorry, more sorry than they could possibly imagine. In time he was reconciled to each one of his children—except Daisy. She vowed she would never speak to him again. Her father's reappearance rattled her badly. Old memories of his drunken rages came flooding back as she lay in bed at night. "He can't undo all that just by saying, 'I'm sorry,'" Daisy insisted. Even though they lived just eight houses down the street from each other, Daisy never once stopped to visit her father, even when he became terminally ill with cancer. He went to his grave with Daisy still carrying her bitterness and anger.

All her life Daisy had determined to be unlike her father, and yet she was as hard as steel. She never apologized and never forgave. An explosive person, she would scream at and verbally abuse her own children. Her daughter Margaret remembers as a child coming in tears to apologize for something she'd done. Daisy responded with a parental Catch 22: "You can't possibly be sorry. If you were really sorry, you wouldn't have done it in the first place."

Margaret went on to be like her mother, Daisy—angry, hard as steel, never apologizing, never forgiving, scolding, threatening. The day came when, in a fit of anger, Margaret ordered her son Michael out of the house. "I never want to see you again as long as I live," she yelled. Twenty-six years later she still hadn't seen his face.

In time Michael mirrored both his mother's and his grand-mother's disposition. Yancey, who knew the family well, tells of a moment when Michael got off the phone with his wife, Sue—they were settling the last financial issues of their divorce. "I hope I never see her again as long as I live," he said in almost the same tone Yancey had heard from Michael's mother, Margaret.

"Like a spiritual defect encoded in the family DNA," writes Yancey, "ungrace gets passed on in an unbroken chain. Ungrace does its work quietly and lethally, like a poisonous, undetectable gas. A father dies unforgiven. A mother who once carried a child in her of body does not speak to that child for half its life. The toxin steals on, from generation to generation." [15] "What is true of families is true also of tribes, races, and nations." [16] And, I will add, even Christian churches—including Seventh-day Adventist congregations.

The cycle of ungrace is a story that stretches endlessly across the landscape of our own personal lives. Each of us lives in a world of ungrace, a tit-for-tat existence in which getting even, holding grudges, and unkindness seems to be the norm. We do not forgive easily, nor do we find ourselves easily forgiven. The fruits of the Spirit—love, joy, peace, patience, kindness, goodness, faithfulness, and gentleness—seem so far from our lives.

"Breaking the cycle of ungrace means *taking the initiative.*" [17] It calls for someone to break the deadlock. Joseph decided that the cycle of ungrace that had been part of the dysfunction of his family for generations was going to come to an end. And the only way that it could cease was for him to wail in forgiveness, and to speak words and extend acts of grace. In this incredible passage we hear the sound of a man forgiving. If we listen carefully, we will hear sounds of grace. Joseph points us to a better way—the way of grace and for-giveness. He held all the cards and could have played them exactly as he wished. His brothers were completely at his mercy. But Joseph ascended out of the pit of ungrace. When we put on his colorful tunic and dream of a people as faithful as he, there before our vision will appear men and women with lives filled with grace—God's grace to them and through them. To everyone who hurts them. Grace alone melts ungrace!

------

[1] N. H. Rosenblatt and J. Horwitz, *Wrestling With Angels,* pp. 363, 364.

[2] G. A. Getz, *Joseph,* p. 166.

[3] F. B. Meyer, *The Life of Joseph,* p. 88.

[4] Getz, p. 166.

[5] Yancy, p. 85.

[6] Elizabeth O'Connor, *Cry Pain, Cry Hope* (Waco, Tex.: Word Books, 1987), p. 167.

[7] P. Yancey, *What's So Amazing About Grace?* pp. 83-93.

[8] L. B. Smedes, *Shame and Grace,* pp. 136, 137.

[9] E. G. White, *Patriarchs and Prophets,* p. 230.

[10] *Ibid.*

[11] Smedes, p. 119.

[12] *Ibid.,* p. 120.

[13] *Ibid.*

[14] *Ibid.,* p. 122.

[15] Yancey, p. 79.

[16] *Ibid.,* p. 81.

[17] *Ibid.,* p. 91.

CHAPTER 13

Do God and Satan Work Alternate Shifts?

GENESIS 45:1-15; 50:15-21

One of my most enjoyable experiences is to drive over a mountain pass containing numerous switchbacks. The grandeur and magnificence of it all just sweeps me away. Our family particularly enjoyed following Wyoming's Route 212 through Beartooth Pass from Red Lodge, Montana, to the northeast entrance of Yellowstone National Park. It was awesome. Another awe-inspiring climb is Going-to-the-Sun Road in Montana's Glacier National Park. Now, that's a highway! Every turn is breathtaking. From one switchback to the next your mind keeps saying it can't get any better than this—but it does.

Mountain switchbacks provide absolutely incredible vistas. As you ascend, you can periodically pull off the highway and look back. There, winding down the mountain and into the valley below, is a ribbon of road curving around a series of hairpin turns. When you begin driving again, however, all you can see is the road a few hundred yards ahead and behind. But as you reach each lookout, you can see the panorama and pattern below. When you finally top the summit, you can tell where you have come from and where you are going. After all that climbing you can see the big picture. It's an awesome experience.

Many of us have come to some point in our life journey when we can look back and gradually, or perhaps suddenly, spot a distinct pattern that we have not noticed before. The events in our lives—particularly the painful ones—make sense for the first time. The twists and turns of our lives come together like interlocking pieces of a puzzle. A divine mosaic emerges. We now see clearly that God has been working in our lives, even when we didn't realize it.

Joseph reached this kind of "aha" point in his life when he looked down and recognized that the 10 men kneeling on the ground before him were his very own brothers. At that pivotal moment he "remembered the dreams which he had about them" (Gen. 42:9). That flashback became a master key in unlocking his understanding of why God had allowed them to sell him into Egypt. Joseph discovered two important truths about God that would forever keep him from the pit of narrow perspective. He learned what God did and what God intended as he grasped how God works in relation to human free will. And he realized why God does what He does the way that He does.

Beyond Our Grasp

Now let me ask you a question. According to the story, who caused Joseph to wind up in Egypt? His brothers or God? Joseph says, "You sold me here," but then he declares, "God sent me" (Gen. 45:5). Again, Joseph adds, "It was not you who sent me here, but God" (verse 8). Who was responsible? Joseph's brothers or God?

One of the questions every one of us asks at some point in our life goes: "If God is in control, are people really free?" It's a question that has bothered Christians for centuries. They have offered lots of answers, but today Christians still disagree. David and Randall Basinger present the dilemma this way:

"The Christian faith presents us with a dilemma. On the one hand, we believe that God made us morally responsible beings with the ability to make meaningful moral decisions. . . . On the other hand, Christians also believe that God has sovereign control over all earthly affairs. He is the Lord of history and the Lord of our lives. . . . The dilemma becomes clear. Can both of these basic Christian beliefs be true? If we are really able to make meaningful moral decisions, then must we not be able to act against God's will? If this is so, then how can we maintain that all that occurs is in keeping with his will? If humans are free, how can God be sovereign? On the other hand, if God is in control, how can human choices be real? In what sense can we be held responsible for actions if God is responsible for everything?"[1]

Tied to this dilemma are some big concepts about God, such as foreknowledge, predestination, providence, and free will. Simply put, foreknowledge has to do with what God knows. Predestination concerns what God decides. And providence brings us to what God does. The puzzling question is How does what God knows, and what God decides, and what God does affect the reality of our free choice?

Joseph's words bring us to the heart of this age-old question. He uses two phrases that keep both sides of truth before us. On the one hand, "You sold me here," but on the other, "God sent me." "You sold me. God sent me." In no way did their responsibility diminish, but equally in no way had the Lord ever lost control of the situation. Later Joseph says, "You meant evil against me, but God meant it for good in order to bring about this present result" (Gen. 50:20). "It was not you who sent me here, but God" (Gen. 45:8).

His words pull back the veil and allow us to see what has been going on behind the scenes. It was not the brothers who sent Joseph to Egypt—it was God. And God had a purpose for it all. Joseph's experience canceled neither human freedom nor God's gracious sovereignty. They are not in conflict, nor are they to be equated. God's will makes use of all human action, but in no way does human choice limit it. Behind all the events and human plans recounted in the story of Joseph lies God's unchanging plan.

Throughout the account we witness a battle between the dream and the "killers of the dream." Joseph had his dreams about the future that infuriated his brothers. The day came when they saw him on the horizon and said, "Here comes this dreamer." At that moment they decided once and for all to kill Joseph. By murdering the dreamer, Joseph's brothers somehow felt they could destroy the dream. "Let's see what becomes of his dreams!" they said to themselves (Gen. 37:20). In the unfolding story, all sorts of enemies of the dream tried to resist its fulfillment—the brothers, Potiphar's wife, the famine. All resisted the dream and failed.[2] The evil plans of human beings were not able to defeat God's purpose. In fact, they unwittingly furthered God's plan.

God oversees people's wicked actions. No sin happens that he doesn't deliberately allow. Don't misunderstand—He is not the source of evil deeds. God never tempts anyone (James 1:13-15).

Rather, God steers the sin already in peoples' hearts so that they (the sinners) unwittingly fulfill His plans and not merely their own. He accomplishes this by infinite wisdom beyond our grasp (Prov. 16:4; Acts 4:28; Gen. 45:7, 8).[3]

God may not initiate all our trials, but by the time those trials reach us, they may have become His will for us. When Satan, other people, or just plain "accidents" bring us sorrow, we can answer as Joseph did to his brothers who had sold him into slavery: "As for you, you meant evil against me, but God meant it for good" (Gen. 50:20).[4]

The book *Education* sums up this incredible truth:

"In the annals of human history the growth of nations, the rise and fall of empires, appear as dependent on the will and prowess of man. The shaping of events seem, to a great degree, to be determined by his power, ambition, or caprice. But in the Word of God the curtain is drawn aside, and we behold, behind, above, and through all the play and counterplay of human interests and power and passions, the agencies of the all-merciful One, silently, patiently working out the counsels of His own will."[5]

Joseph's story hinges on the conviction that God is freely at work for His purpose in spite of, through, and against every human effort.[6] "God's purposes are worked out *in concrete history* through the actions of identifiable persons."[7] The dream had been at work all along, not in the least diminished by the morality of any of the characters in the story.[8] God's providence, however, did not lessen the moral responsibility of those involved.

But What Is He Up To?

In 1985 Frank Slazak had an opportunity to compete in NASA's Teacher in Space program. Ever since he had been a boy Slazak had dreamed of being an astronaut. But he lived in a little conservative coal mining town with a very limited view of the world and wound up doing what many other young people did. He graduated from high school and college and taught science just eight miles from where he was born. But his dream of flying in space never died. Then it happened! In early 1985, like a lightning bolt from the sky, the White House announced that President Reagan was directing NASA to begin the search for an ordinary citizen to fly on board a space shuttle mission. Reagan further specified that the person would be a teacher. Slazak was a teacher and an ordinary citizen, so he applied. And waited and prayed, going out to the mailbox day after day. More than 43,000 individuals requested applications. Eleven thousand actually submitted them. What were his chances? But the day came when an official-looking envelope with NASA's logo on it arrived. He was down to an elite group of less than 100. Slazak went through the training process with high hopes. Then came the devastating news. He would not be the first teacher to fly in space. NASA had chosen someone else named Christa McAuliffe. His lifelong dream was over. Depression, loss of confidence, and anger replaced his euphoria as he questioned everything: "Why God, why not me? What part of the right stuff did I lack? Why has life dealt me such a cruel blow? How can I face my students, my family, and my community who have encouraged me on? Why did my dream have to end when I was so close?" Filled with pain, Slazak felt as if he were dying inside. He just didn't understand.

Tuesday, January 28, 1986, the day Slazak had dreamed about for 25 years, found him gathered with those who had shared his failed dream at Kennedy Space Center. He had come to witness the historic flight of teacher Christa McAuliffe. Slazak watched as the space shuttle *Challenger* lifted off the launch pad on what seemed like a perfect launch. As it cleared that launch tower, Slazak challenged his dream one final time. "God, I would do anything to be in that shuttle. Why can't that be me?"

Seventy-three seconds later God answered all his questions and invalidated all his doubts as *Challenger* exploded, killing all on board, including teacher Christa McAuliffe. He realized then and there that he had not been chosen for that flight because God's plan for him was better.[9]

Joseph also learned what God intended, and why God does the things the way that He does. Thus he could declare, "You meant it evil against me, but God meant it for good." The New International Version uses "intended." Realizing what God has been doing, Joseph places the "intention" of the brothers over against the "intention" of God (Gen. 50:20). Although the brothers intended evil, God intended good. The brothers sought death for one while God desired life for many. The intention of God prevailed over, worked through, circumvented the intention of the brothers. Scripture does not tell us how God accomplished it, but He did. It gives us a glimpse into how God works His divine intention amid the human drama.[10]

According to Joseph, God's intention was clear: "For God sent me before you to preserve life. . . . God sent me before you to preserve for you a remnant in the earth, and to keep you alive by a great deliverance" (Gen. 45:5-7). The sovereign providence of God ultimately concerns life and death, preserving a remnant, bringing a great deliverance. His purposes have been at work in, with, and under the sordid human actions. Joseph's words announce unambiguously that God wills and works life for His people and the people of the earth. The technical terms *remnant* and *survivors* assure that there will be a future despite heavy odds.[11]

Joseph undoubtedly grasped the larger picture. "God will surely take care of you, and bring you up from this land to the land which He promised on oath to Abraham, to Isaac and to Jacob" (Gen. 50:24).

Genesis portrays Joseph as the imperial power broker who controlled the course of events. In the process he led his brothers toward an awakened conscience, repentance of sin, and the desire for grace. Graciously he forgave and gave them grace rather than the ungrace they expected. The story ends with them all speaking together. Joseph's own actions mirror God's intent to lead us to Himself, awakening our conscience to forgotten and unforgiven sins, graciously forgiving them, sovereignly preserving our life, ultimately reuniting us with Himself, and settling us in a good land where He will nourish us for eternity.

"You meant evil against me, but God meant it for good" (Gen. 50:20). "God causes all things to work together for good to those who love God, to those who are called according to His purpose" (Rom. 8:28).

Sometimes we can feel as if God and Satan work alternate shifts. Or that Satan is busy most, if not all, shifts. But Joseph's incredible experience denies that possibility. Furthermore, it teaches us three wonderful truths about God:[12]

  1. God is love: His will is always best. In fact, His very nature is

love (1 John 4:16). He will never act in a way contrary to His own nature. Never in our life will God ever express His will toward us except as it reflects His perfect love for us. That love always seeks the very best for us. He will never give us second best. "'I know the plans that I have for you,' declares the Lord, 'plans for welfare and not for calamity to give you a future and a hope'" (Jer. 29:11).

2. God is all-knowing: His leading is always right. By nature He possesses all knowledge—past, present, future. Nothing is outside the sphere of His knowledge. God can see the end from the beginning, from cause to effect. He understands the ins and outs of every situation and the moral and spiritual issues at stake. Everything there is to know about me and you and our temporal and eternal welfare. Whenever God leads us, His providence is always the right path for us. Before He ever gives us a directive, we can count on the fact that He has already considered every factor. We will never follow His leading and find out later that He must have been mistaken. "God is greater than our heart, and knows all things" (1 John 3:20). His law "is perfect, restoring the soul; the testimony of the Lord is sure, making wise the simple (Ps. 19:7). "It is He who reveals the profound and hidden things; He knows what is in the darkness, and the light dwells with Him" (Dan. 2:22). "I am God, and there is no other; I am God, and there is no one like Me, declaring the end from the beginning and from ancient times things which have not been done" (Isa. 46:9, 10).

3. God is all-powerful: He can enable us to accomplish His will. And He will succeed for us. The Lord can accomplish anything He purposes to do. In fact He says, "'My purpose will be established, and I will accomplish all My good pleasure.' . . . Truly I have spoken; truly I will bring it to pass. I have planned it, surely I will do it" (Isa. 46:10, 11). If He ever asks us to do something, we can be sure He will enable us to do it. Sometimes, like Joseph, we face the humanly impossible. It is at those moments that God says, "Just let me be God. Turn to me for your needed power, insight, skill, resources. I will give you everything you need." As the apostle Paul learned, "I can do all things through Him who strengthens me" (Phil. 4:13). God will enable us to accomplish all that He calls us to do.

What we believe about God and His involvement in our lives

should make a difference as to how we face difficult circumstances. As Corrie ten Boom said: "Never be afraid to trust an unknown future to a known God." Even the atheistic philosopher Nietzsche understood the issue: "He who has a *why* to live can bear with almost any *how.*"

Viktor Frankl writes how in the concentration camp every circumstance conspired to make the prisoners lose their hold. It snatched away all familiar goals in life. And yet, even under such extreme psychic and physical stress, one can still decide what shall become of oneself mentally and spiritually:

"We who lived in concentration camps can remember men who walked through the huts comforting others, giving away their last piece of bread. They may have been few in number, but they offer sufficient proof that everything can be taken from a man but one thing: the last of human freedoms—to choose one's attitude in any given set of circumstances, to choose one's own way."[13]

We can trust the future because of God's intention. God's providence is moral[14] and fueled by a heart of gracious love. When we know Him, we will never have to sense emptiness or fear or lack of purpose. He will always fill our life with Himself. When we have Him, we have everything there is.

---

[1] David Basinger and Randall Basinger, eds., *Predestination and Free Will: Four Views of Divine Sovereignty & Human Freedom* (Downers Grove, Ill.: InterVarsity press, 1986), p. 7.

[2] W. Brueggemann, *Genesis,* p. 301.

[3] J. E. Tada and S. Estes, *When God Weeps,* p. 222.

[4] *Ibid.*

[5] Ellen G. White, *Education* (Mountain View, Calif.: Pacific Press Pub. Assn., 1952), p. 173.

[6] Brueggemann, p. 346.

[7] *Ibid.,* p. 348.

[8] *Ibid.,* p. 371.

[9] Frank Slazak, "I Won Because I Lost," and *A Third Serving of Chicken Soup for the Soul* (Deerfield Beach, Fla.: Health Communications, Inc., 1996), pp. 225-229.

[10] E. F. Roop, *Genesis,* p. 291.

[11] Brueggemann, p. 346.

[12] I have adapted the following points from Henry T. Blackaby and Claude V. King's *Experiencing God,* pp. 17-27.

[13] V. E. Frankl, *Man's Search for Meaning,* p. 86.

[14] W. M. Taylor, *Joseph the Prime Minister,* p. 239.

CHAPTER 14

Sidetracked? Or Awaiting the Visit?

GENESIS 50:22-25

had heard of El Al's tight security, but I never dreamed I would spend nearly an hour answering questions before being allowed to move on to the airline check-in counter. And I was still in the U.S.! Yet, I stood in front of a serious-faced security officer with a peach-fuzz goatee. Despite his obvious youth, the sandy-haired fellow exuded an air of authority and played his role well. As he asked me all kinds of personal questions—who I was, why I was traveling to Israel, who paid for my ticket, how long I would stay in Israel, whether I had any Arab friends, who I knew in Israel, whether anyone else was traveling with me, whether I had ever been to Israel before—he made no eye contact whatsoever. He was detached, suspicious, impersonal. Mater-of-factly professional. Thoroughly absorbed in skillfully determining whether I was any threat to the nation of Israel. But I sidetracked him with a simple story!

Somewhere in the process I had told him I was traveling to Jerusalem to read a scholarly paper at a Bible conference. After a while he abruptly came back to that answer and asked to see the paper. When I handed it to him, he scanned the cover page for a fraction of a second. Then, never even looking at me, he asked mechanically, "What is your conclusion? How do you end this paper?" My mind whirled for a moment, trying to make the mental leap from the concise mater-of-fact answers I had been giving to encapsulating my academic conclusion in a nutshell of an answer.

I began with the closing story I used of a time management expert making a point with a group of business students. He had pulled out a one-gallon, widemouthed mason jar and carefully filled it with a dozen fist-sized rocks. When he had put rocks in up to the rim and no more would fit inside, he asked, "Is the jar full?"

Everyone in the class said yes.

"Really?" he said, as he reached under the table and pulled out a bucket of gravel. By shaking the jar as he poured in the gravel, he was able to fill in the spaces between the big rocks.

"Is the jar full?" he asked again.

"Probably not," someone cautiously replied.

Then he poured in some sand, and with some shaking of the jar it slipped into all the spaces left between the rocks and gravel. "Is the jar full?"

They were on to him now. "No!" the class shouted.

Now he produced a pitcher of water and began to pour it in until the jar was full to the brim. Finally he looked up at the class and asked, "What is the point of this illustration?"

One eager beaver raised his hand and said, "The point is, no matter how full your schedule is, if you try really hard, you can always fit more things into it."

"No," the speaker replied, "that's not the point. The truth this illustration teaches us is that if you don't put the big rocks in first, you'll never get them all in."

"And so," I concluded, "if we don't care for the really important moral spiritual issues in our life first, we'll have problems relating to them later. And all the rest of life will mean diddly-squat."

As I related this story, I kept thinking to myself, *This guy isn't really interested in anything I'm saying. He's just trying to see if I know what I wrote. If it was really my paper.* But when I got to the punch line, he looked up at me for the very first time and with a far-off expression in his eyes said, "That's so true, isn't it? This is in the Bible?"

"No, the story is not in the Bible," I replied, "but putting the rocks in first shows the fundamental need for filling our moral vision with perspectives from God's Word before all else."

I have no idea what clicked in the security agent's mind. Nor what was going on in his life. But for a brief moment we had a personal exchange about the importance of caring for the really vital things in life. He was no longer a security agent and I a potential danger to his country. We were two human beings talking about real life.

Joseph had made sure all the big rocks were in place early in his life. As a result, he never lost sight of the grand dream and wonderful promise God had for His people. Nor was Joseph ever unwittingly sidetracked by Egypt's powerful culture and values.

We can read it clearly in the text. The closing words of Genesis begin with Joseph living "in Egypt" (Gen. 50:22), then dying "in Egypt" (verse 26). In between these two references to Egypt, however, is the never-failing vision of God's incredible promise for His people. That someday He would visit His people. "God will surely visit you . . ." the passage reads (verses 24, 25, NKJV). Egypt may frame the last recorded moments of Joseph's life, but the viewpoint is God's gracious visit and the land of promise. The passage juxtaposes the land of Egypt and the land of promise, puts them side by side. After living 93 years in Egypt—and most of it in the elite level of society—the heart of Joseph is still fully Israelite and still tuned to God's blessing. Joseph lived in Egypt, but he never became one with Egypt. He was *in* his world, but not *of* his world. The dream of God's promised visit and final blessing to God's people never grew dim or faded. Hope had not died. Joseph never succumbed to the pit of lost dreams.

Oriented in Moral Space

For a moment the serious-minded El Al security officer forgot who he was. Ignoring the work he was supposed to be doing, he found himself caught up in another world altogether. Such is the power of stories. By capturing our interest, holding our attention, and stirring emotions, they help us remember. They impact us in ways that precepts and propositions never do. Their meaning slips past our conscious mind and its defenses to touch us on a level we can't explain.

The same happens with world culture at large! Our world of culture is a paradigmatic story in and of itself. And like most paradigms, culture consists of multiple supporting stories. Each of the tangible expressions of contemporary culture (our world), no matter the milieu of time or specific context, have a way of capturing us. Whether it be the arts, music, architecture, customs and lifestyle, habits, values, beliefs, or ways of looking at life—each in its own way tells a story, creates a worldview. Each has an uncanny way of slipping past our conscious mind, circumventing our defenses, and sidetracking us. Culture can divert us to the point that we forget who we are and what we are supposed to be doing for God in the world—both individually and as an end-time remnant people.

While we cannot always define the "essence" of culture, it is inextricably bound up with human life in society. Culture at bottom is social.[1] The world of culture is a realm of values concerned with what is good for human beings.[2] In all its forms and varieties culture seeks the temporal and material realization of those values.[3] "Don't let the world around you squeeze you into its own mould, but let God re-make you so that your whole attitude of mind is changed," Paul exclaims (Rom. 12:2, Phillips). Our problem today is that all too many of us have become sidetracked by Egypt—squeezed into the world's mold.

We're living in a period of time Peter described as the last days when scoffers would demand, "Where is the promise of His coming?" (2 Peter 3:3, 4). Ever since the beginning of time, history has come and gone, and He's not come yet. Where is He?

Today, as the book of Hebrews says, many need encouragement to hold fast to the dream. "Let us hold fast the profession of our hope without wavering, for He who promised is faithful" (Heb. 10:23). "Do not throw away your confidence, which has a great reward. For you have need of endurance, so that when you have done the will of God, you may receive what was promised. For yet in a very little while, He who is coming will come, and will not delay. But My righteous one shall live by faith; and if he shrinks back, My soul has no pleasure in him. But we are not of those who shrink back to destruction, but of those who have faith to the preserving of the soul" (verses 35-39). Many at the time Hebrews was written were letting go, allowing the things they had heard about redemption through Jesus drift away (Heb. 2:1). We are no different. Today many of us need to hear the call to persevere, to endure, to hang on, to firmly grasp our hope in Jesus and not shrink back.

Jesus, too, spoke about lost dreams: "Be on guard, that your hearts may not be weighted down with dissipation and drunkenness and the worries of life, and that day come on you suddenly like a trap; for it will come upon all those who dwell on the face of all the earth. But keep on the alert at all times, praying in order that you may have strength to escape all these things that are about to take place, and to stand before the Son of Man" (Luke 21:34-36). And the apostle John invites us to "abide in Him, so that when He appears, we may have confidence and not shrink away from Him in shame at His coming" (1 John 2:28).

Why does Scripture repeat this theme again and again? Simple! So often the dream fades. The hope dies. People lose a sense of who they are and what they are to be doing in the world. They become part of Egypt—*in* the world and very much *of* it.

Joseph knew the pressure of forgetting the dream. He understood the whirlwind that lashes us when we get caught up in the temporal and material reality of our world. The patriarch came to Egypt during Egypt's great Middle Kingdom. A number of scholars place Joseph in the Twelfth Dynasty, and he may have lived during the reigns of four pharaohs. If so, he was in Egypt during the last years of Amenemhat II and the subsequent reigns of Sesostris II, the great Sesostris III, and finally Amenemhat III (roughly 1902-1809 B.C.).[4] Thus Joseph probably saw four Pharaohs come and go.

The Twelfth Dynasty was a time of extensive foreign trade and great military conquests. It was a period of creative development in literature, the arts, and massive architecture. The Middle Kingdom was truly a great time for Egypt. The architecture, art, sculpture, statuary, forts, temples, and paintings all witness to the skill of the nation's craftspeople.[5] Inscriptions and reliefs, all brightly colored, decorated the walls, ceilings, and columns of their buildings. Not only were the interiors of Egyptian buildings and temples covered with painted reliefs and inscriptions, but all the outer walls as well, including the towered gateways. In fact, the public buildings, temples, and palaces alike literally blazed with color.

Even today, when you stand in the temple of Karnak at Thebes—one of the glorious religious and political centers of ancient Egypt near the famed Valley of the Kings—its splendor can overwhelm you. Here you are, centuries later, looking at ruins—ruins mind you—yet you cannot but help stand in awe as you look down an impressive corridor that seems to have no end. Massive pillars vault each side. Some of the colors still remain after thousands of years.

Its creators designed all this grand culture to capture your soul. Arrest your interest. Stir your emotions. Tell you a story. Win you deep down inside. Conform you to its own image. Squeeze you into its mold. In sum, make you Egyptian.

Joseph knew this magnificent world culture and its enchantment. And yet, in the end, Egypt held no attraction. As we have already learned, Joseph was "exposed to temptations of no ordinary character. He was in the midst of idolatry. The worship of false gods was surrounded by all the pomp of royalty, supported by the wealth and culture of the most highly civilized nation then in existence. Yet Joseph preserved his simplicity and his fidelity to God. The sights and sounds of vice were all about him, but he was as one who saw and heard not. His thoughts were not permitted to linger upon forbidden subjects."[6]

No matter his station in life—slave, steward, prisoner, prime minister, father—Joseph was "a man for all seasons," God's faithful friend and servant. Always he heard God's story in his heart no matter what Egypt whispered in his ears.

Genesis tells us that as they lived in Egypt the children of Israel accumulated possessions and grew in number (Gen. 47:27; Ex. 1:7). The possibility of being absorbed into Egyptian culture was great. Joseph, however, had wisely placed his family in Goshen, somewhat removed from the rest of Egypt (Gen. 46:28-34). It "would enable them to remain a distinct and separate people and would thus serve to shut them from participation in the idolatry of Egypt."[7] Notice what five of Joseph's brothers said to Pharaoh when they visited the palace: "We have come to sojourn in the land ["to reside as aliens" (NRSV)]" (Gen. 47:4). They were careful to state that they had come only for a while and were not seeking permanent residence.[8] No, they weren't supposed to settle in for the long haul or become like the Egyptians, who personified civilized culture. Joseph wanted them to maintain their identity and character as God's people even as they lived in Egypt.

In his book *Sources of the Self* Charles Taylor writes: "To know who you are is to be oriented in moral space, a space in which questions arise about what is good or bad, what is worth doing and what not, what has meaning and importance for you and what is trivial and secondary."[9]

"To know who you are is to be oriented in moral space." David Wells suggests that the flip side is also true, i.e., "not to be oriented in moral space is not to know who you are. This is the situation that is assuming epidemic proportions in our postmodern world."[10] To be dislodged from moral space is to lose one's identity. That's what's happening in our world today. The collapse of belief in our post-modern world expresses itself in two crucial features—pluralism of authority, and the centrality of choice.[11] Pluralism of authority simply means the apparent absence of any universal authority. It rules out the setting of binding norms that all moral agents must obey. In effect, this places moral responsibility wholly upon individuals who now must face point-blank the consequences of their actions. Eminent sociologist and postmodern theorist Zygmunt Bauman encapsulates the postmodern condition well:

"The ethical paradox of the postmodern condition is that it restores to agents the fullness of moral choice and responsibility while simultaneously depriving them of the comfort of the universal guidance that modern self-confidence once promised. Ethical tasks of individuals grow while the socially produced resources to fulfill them shrink. Moral responsibility comes together with the loneliness of moral choice. In a cacophony of moral voices, none which is likely to silence the others, the individuals are thrown back on their own subjectivity as the only ultimate ethical authority. At the same time, however, they are told repeatedly about the irreparable relativism of any moral code."[12]

In essence, "we are losing both the moral fabric of life and our own identity as moral beings."[13]

"To know who you are is to be oriented in moral space." Personal identity, then, is not simply a matter of mental awareness, or mere data about one's self—name, gender, race, religion, weight, eye color, occupation. It has to do with character—where we both identify ourselves and "are" morally and spiritually. Furthermore, personal identity has to do with those things that make us continuous with who we were yesterday, last month, or 10 years ago. The ability to preserve our personal identity in the midst of a changing world—or a world that would squeeze us unto its mold—results from the rootedness of character in our way of being. A long period of consistent obedience creates a reservoir of moral orientation, and subsequently of identity.

Wells writes that "what strengthens the sense of identity . . . are those things that require a person to be continuous with who he or she was."[14] To illustrate this, he refers to the matter of promise. At their heart, all promises bind the person who makes them to be the same person in the future as the one who is doing the promising in the present. When an individual makes a promise the future often lies still unopened. As it unfolds, moment by moment, the person comes to see what it actually requires to keep the promise. One's intent to be the same person as the one who made the promise will be tested through misunderstanding, moral failures, illness, and the pressures of modern life. It is the keeping of the promise, however, that forges identity. In a curious paradox, the self-restraint and self-control that are inevitably a part of keeping a promise are the very means of strengthening the self, rather than diminishing it. Wells concludes:

"Where a promise is kept, there is an unbreached moral relationship between the person who makes the promise and the person who receives it. What sustains that continuity, and what therefore underwrites a sense of identity, is the very thing most imperiled in the postmodern world: moral principle."[15]

Egypt would create a new moral frame of reference. In associating too closely with their Egyptian world and culture, God's people's risked losing both the moral fabric of their life and their own moral and spiritual identity. Our postmodern world threatens our own identity as moral beings. We experience it as God's people today. "Who are we?" some Seventh-day Adventists ask today. Our world is changing, and for some of us, our identity alters with it. I believe there's a call here in this passage to make sure the big rocks are well placed in the moral/spiritual jar of our hearts. The big rocks need to be there, or we will loose our identity. Those big rocks include our relationship with Jesus Christ and the full assurance of sins forgiven and the indwelling of His Holy Spirit; the literal reading and meaning of Genesis 1-11 as accounts of earth's origin and early history (including creation in six literal 24-hour periods and a world-wide flood); the seventh-day Sabbath as a sign of our forever friendship with the Creator God; the human condition in death and the truth that life is found only in the resurrected Lord; the high priestly ministry of Jesus in the heavenly sanctuary; and the pre-Advent judgment and soon return of Jesus Christ. If we ever lose sight of that promise of God's final visit, and of a final blessing in a Promised Land, everything else will be meaningless.

David and Marian Lewis were two Adventist young people who had lost the dream. Somewhere along the way they became disconnected from Jesus, detached from their heritage as Bible-believing Adventist Christians. They got caught up in the story of our world culture and all that it whispered in their ears. Marian headed off to high fashion, becoming a noted print, runway, and commercial model, doing gigs for Bob Mackey, Liz Claiborne, Valentino, and Oil of Olay. Driven by the image of the Beatles with girls screaming, pulling out their hair, and fainting, David's passion was to become a recording artist who would enthrall audiences and sell millions of CDs. He was lead singer/writer of the pop group Atlantic Starr. Both he and Marian headed down the fast lane, immersed in the applause, the money, the culture that contemporary Egypt provides.

David and Marian met during an interview for her to sing with Atlanta Starr. Cruising Manhattan together in David's red 635 BMW, their conversation turned from business to common experiences, including a shared childhood in the Seventh-day Adventist Church—the church each of them had left behind. In time they married. And also in time they realized that the direction of their lives, the compromises, the emptiness, and the stress were just not worth it. Having lost their moral framework and identity, they wanted something more. Through God's leading they found themselves once again in a baptismal pool and now are telling the wonderful story of how God has reignited the dream.

What fascinates me is that here's a superstar couple who have been there, done that. They have done things, owned things, and been things that most of us will never experience in our whole life. And when you asked them about music, or Christian lifestyle, or

142

dress standards—issues that some of us feel are of no moral/spiritual consequence anymore—they candidly answered that their walk with Jesus was their first passion now. Certain things are no longer appropriate or cannot nurture that relationship with Christ.

Since leaving Atlantic Starr, David has rejected lucrative offers to return to pop music. "There's always going to be somebody trying to redirect your vision" he says.[16] Vision—that's what it's all about. God's dream or Egypt's dream. Which is it for you?

Joseph never for a moment forgot who he was or what he was doing for God in an idolatrous world filled with emptiness, fear, sorrow, and darkness. We too must never forget our identity. Never forget that we are catalysts whom God will use to change people's worldview in the final hours of history (Rev. 14:6-12; 18:1-5). And never forget that we are a remnant with a unique mission in a raging conflict between Christ and Satan. A people with a vibrant hope in the soon and glorious return of Jesus Christ. And a people in a forever friendship with Jesus.

God Will Surely Visit

Behind Joseph's steadfastness was the purpose, providence, and promise of God. "God will *surely* visit you" (Gen. 50:24, 25, NKJV). Twice he says it. That wonderful hope of divine visit rests on God's promise. He swore it to Abraham, to Isaac, and to Jacob. You can count on it. God has sworn His word—and keeps it. But first comes a time of waiting.[17] We can hold on to a dream when the One who promised is trustworthy (Heb. 10:23). That's why Hebrews tells us, "By faith Joseph, when he was dying, made mention of the departure of the children of Israel, and gave instructions concerning his bones" (Heb. 11:22, NKJV). In his dying words Joseph gave instructions about his body, because he had in his mind, by faith, the departure of the children of Israel from Egypt. The word of God declares that the day will come when the people of God will again depart from the world of Egypt. Those who hold that blessed dream dear in their heart have endured anxious waiting for the first sign of Christ's appearing (Rom. 8:19). God was real to Joseph. And because God was real to him, he believed what God said both about the visit and departure.

So the story of Joseph and the book of Genesis end in Egypt, awaiting the visit. "The visit of God creates possibility for another beginning."[18]

For some of us, the dream is fading, our hope dying. What is there to do about it? Because God will surely come, whether we believe it or not.

As a young boy, Ty Gibson had a quick mind and a sharp memory. His teachers said he was a gifted child with lots of potential. But he quickly squandered and abused his mental gift. In the fifth grade Ty and his friends began taking Valium in the restrooms during recess. The next year he smoked marijuana almost every day after school. By the seventh grade he was snorting cocaine and experimenting with LSD. His days at school consisted mainly of drug deals and party plans. Soon Ty could barely remember his own address, and reading became hard labor. He had fried his brain.

Through a remarkable series of providences God graciously won this young man to Himself, eventually leading him to become a Seventh-day Adventist Christian at the age of 18. Then it hit Ty with full force just how he had been destroying himself and how much he had wasted of his mind. Ty tried to read, to remember, and to comprehend the great truths of Scripture, but it seemed so elusive, so impossible. One day he made a bargain with the Lord. He had learned about the principles of stewardship at an evangelistic meeting: Return one tenth of your income to the Lord, and He will open the windows of heaven and pour out a blessing beyond what you have room to receive. *Perhaps the Lord might do that with my mind,* Ty thought. So he made a bargain with the Lord. "Lord, I'm going to give You a tenth of my time. Out of every 24-hour period, I'm going to give You two and a half hours. I'm going to read the Bible. I'm going to study. My mind needs to be healed."

For the next 18 months Ty kept his end of the bargain. Every day he spent a tenth of his time reading and praying over Scripture until he began to find his mind beginning to work and think and dream and be connected again. In that experience he also became personally acquainted with God's beautiful character. It's a marvelous testimony of God's grace and how Scripture can heal the mind. Scripture has healing power.[19]

If your hope has died, if the dream has faded from your heart, it's time to immerse yourself again in the Word of God. Be confronted again with the dream—the dream of God's love, final blessing, and final redemptive visit. Only in this way will the dream grow and become a vital part of your sense of reality.

"To know who we are is to be oriented in moral space." Hearing God's story orients us in His moral space and gives us rock-solid identity even as Egypt whispers its story in our ears.

------

[1] H. Richard Niebuhr, *Christ and Culture* (New York: Harper and Row, 1975), p. 32.

[2] *Ibid.,* pp. 34, 35.

[3] *Ibid.,* p. 36.

[4] "As to Joseph's exact date within the Middle Kingdom, James R. Battenfield has collated the biblical information with the accepted chronology of the Middle Kingdom. In summary, Joseph was sold into slavery in approximately 1897 B.C., during the last years of Amenemhat II. It was then Sesostris II who first imprisoned and later elevated Joseph to a position of power in about 1884 B.C.; but since that pharaoh died in 1878, the bulk of Joseph's career belongs to the reign of the great king Sesostris III" (Charles F. Aling, *Egypt and Bible History* [Grand Rapids: Baker Book House, 1981], p. 30). Adventist archaeologists place Joseph's entrance into Egypt in 1902 B.C. See Paul J. Ray, "The Duration of the Israelite Sojourn in Egypt," *AUSS,* Autumn 1986, pp. 231-248.

[5] Aling, p. 27.

[6] E. G. White, *Patriarchs and Prophets,* p. 214.

[7] *Ibid.,* p. 232.

[8] *Ibid.,* p. 233.

[9] Charles Taylor, *Sources of the Self: The Making of the Modern Identity* (Cambridge, Mass.: Harvard University Press, 1989), p. 28.

[10] David E. Wells, *Losing Our Virtue: Why the Church Must Recover Its Moral Vision* (Grand Rapids: William B. Eerdmans Pub. Co., 1998), p. 141.

[11] Zygmunt Bauman, *Intimations of Postmodernity* (New York: Routledge, 1992), p. 201.

[12] *Ibid.,* p. xxii.

[13] Wells, p. 145.

[14] *Ibid.,* p. 144.

[15] *Ibid.,* p. 145.

[16] Andy Nash, "Always . . . and Forever," *Adventist Review,* June 18, 1998, pp. 8-12.

[17] W. Brueggemann, *Genesis,* p. 379.

[18] *Ibid.*

[19] Ty Gibson, "The Healing Power of Scripture," in *Over & Over Again!* ed. Ronald Alan Knott (Silver Spring, Md.: North American Division of Seventh-day Adventists, 1998), pp. 19, 20.

CHAPTER 15

The End of the Beginning or What to Say When You Arrive at the Hall of the Two Truths

GENESIS 50:22-26

To the ancient Egyptians, death was a dark river, an underground Nile. Its dismal waters bore the deceased away to endless night . . . or to a shining elsewhere of immortal life. They believed that their spiritual survival depended absolutely on their bodies' physical survival—only the mummified could reach immortality[1]—so they lavished a good deal of ingenuity on the art of preserving dead bodies. Whatever your status on earth—pharaoh, commoner, slave—participation in the afterlife depended on three basic things. First, your body must remain intact; second, your name should continue to exist; and third, someone must continue to supply you with food and drink.[2]

Keeping the body intact was a matter of correct embalming and burial procedure. It meant wrapping the body well and placing it in a nest of coffins, during some periods finally protected by a heavy stone sarcophagus. It also included tucking a series of magic charms (amulets) in between the linen wrappings. Scarab amulets were extremely important.[3] They were shaped like the Egyptian dung beetle, which lays its eggs in little bits of dung and then rolls them into perfect spheres. To the Egyptians, the sight of newly hatched beetles emerging from a ball of dung looked like magic—a kind of spontaneous generation. They saw a parallel between the ball of dung being rolled along the ground and the sun passing across the heavens, and so conceived of the beetle god assisting the dead to pass through darkness into the next world. Scarabs guaranteed the wearer new life and resurrection. In addition, the Egyptians would write on papyri or inside the coffin selections from the famous Egyptian collection of spells, the Book of the Dead.

146

Ensuring that your name would last was a comparatively simple matter. You had it carved, written, or painted just about anywhere convenient: on your possessions, your coffins, your sarcophagus, your tomb walls, or the jewelry that adorned your corpse.[4]

Guaranteeing your supply of food and drink for the other world was a question of taking with you the necessary equipment (sickles, hoes, and other tools) and/or the right symbolic equipment such as shabtis (statuettes shaped like mummies that would do the required work for you in the next life) and wooden models depicting servants, craftspeople, and laborers, who would run your farms and industries.[5] Also, you would endow a mortuary temple or cult to offer sacrifices to you after death.

The Egyptian view of the underworld included a whole series of traps and pitfalls for the unprepared. The deceased could evade such dangers only if their spirit knew the correct procedure to follow and the appropriate speeches to recite at certain points in its journey. The answers were all contained in the chapters of the Book of the Dead. All the deceased had to do in order to reach their goal was to follow the instructions laid down in that book. Traveling to the next world was very much like taking an examination with prior knowledge of all the questions and a supply of well-prepared answers. Magical spells were indispensable.[6]

An important moment in the journey to the next world was the judgment. Chapter 125 of the Book of the Dead describes how the deceased would have his or her heart weighed in a balance against the feather of Maat, the goddess of truth and justice. The jackal-headed god Anubis placed the heart in the left-hand pan of the balance and the feather of Maat on the right. Anubis conducted the weighing and Thoth, the scribe of the gods, recorded the result. Behind Anibus crouched the monster Ammit, a crocodile-headed creature with paws like a lion and the hindquarters of a hippopotamus. Ammit's name meant "Eater of the Dead," and his function was to devour the hearts of those who failed to pass the test. They would then die what the Egyptians called the second death.

Chapter 125 also tells of the deceased being examined by 42 different gods who one by one heard the "Negative Confessions."

When the dead arrived at the Hall of the Two Truths, they knew exactly what to say to these gods:

"I have not acted evilly towards anyone; I have not impoverished associates; I have not done evil instead of righteousness . . . I have not committed sins. . . . I have not reviled the god. I have not robbed the orphan, nor have I done what the god detests. I have not slandered a servant to his master. I have not made anyone miserable, nor have I made anyone weep. I have not killed, nor have I ordered anyone to execution. I have not made anyone suffer. I have not diminished the food offerings in the temples, nor have I damaged the bread-offerings of the gods. I have not stolen the cakes of the blessed. I have not copulated [unlawfully], nor have I indulged in fornication. I have not increased nor diminished the measure: I have not diminished the palm. I have not encroached on fields. I have not added to the weights in the balance. I have not taken milk from a child's mouth. . . . I have not opposed the god at his processions."[7]

The person undergoing the test did not await the decision of the gods meekly. They would boldly proclaim their righteousness. They effectively demanded access to Paradise as a right rather than a privilege.[8] The deceased never really confessed anything. Instead, they simply enumerated their virtues.

More than any other early civilization, ancient Egyptian culture was preoccupied with death. Because they enjoyed life so much, they spent it preparing for that mysterious transition to unending life. Failure to make the necessary preparations would result in total annihilation from memory, something the Egyptians feared the most.

A New Genesis

It is in this kind of setting that Joseph dies! It's a simple record. They embalmed him and placed him in a coffin—in Egypt (Gen. 50:26). So Genesis ends with Joseph mummified, encased in one of those colorfully decorated body-shaped coffins. It is interesting how after living in the midst of a virtual kingdom of the dead, Joseph, too, is concerned about his bones and the afterlife. Even about the importance of where they placed his body. "God will surely . . . bring you up from this land to the land which He promised on oath to Abraham, to Isaac and to Jacob. . . . And you shall carry my bones up from here" (Gen. 50:24, 25).

But Joseph's hope was not in magical spells or a carefully preserved body. His confidence did not rest in scarabs or a massive sarcophagus hidden in some secret tomb. Nor was his hope in having his name etched multiplied times in stone or carefully written on his coffin or on papyri placed in his mummified hands. Joseph wasn't looking for stockpiles of food to sustain him in his journey or symbolic boats to help him cross the dismal waters of the underground Nile. He didn't need the Book of the Dead to help him know what to say to the gods assessing his heart in the Hall of the Two Truths. No, Joseph's hope was the Creator-God who could bring order out of chaos and life out of dust (Gen. 1; 2:7). That was his heritage, his hope, and an incredible truth that Egyptian culture refused to believe.

As Eugene Peterson writes: "No life is complete until there is death. Death sets limits. To be human is to die. By dying, we attest to our humanity. Death doesn't so much terminate our humanity as prove it."[9]

Genesis tells us that the original temptation was to try to be like God (Gen. 3:5). The original warning was that if we attempted it, we would die (Gen. 2:16, 17; 3:3). The fact is, we all try it, and we all die. Death, then, "protects and guarantees our humanity. Our attempt to be more than human or other than human (which is the common mark of sin) results in our becoming less than human" (Gen. 3:22-24).[10]

In his arresting book *Why Do Christians Find It Hard to Grieve?* Baptist pastor Geoff Walters points out how even Christians have come to deny death:[11] "Christians find it hard to grieve because, like everyone else, they have an inbuilt tendency to deny the truth about death. Human beings fear death and cover their fear with denial."[12]

Walters sees the problem in a theology of death that rejects its reality—the Plato-Augustinian synthesis of the immortality of the soul that displaces the biblical emphasis on the resurrection of the body when Jesus comes. According to him, belief in the immortality of the soul actually inhibits or suppresses genuine grief. It cuts across the grain of the reality of human response in the wake of such loss. On the other hand, he posits, the biblical teaching—that death is real and that the Christian's only hope is the resurrection—is the most therapeutically effective. It gives space for grief and is perfectly in tune with the contemporary understanding of what grief is and how it works.[13]

Walters proposes, then, a five-point theology of grief:

First, it must be based on a biblical view of the creation of human beings according to Genesis 2:7, in which human beings do not receive a soul but become a "living soul," something inexpressible apart from the body.[14]

Second, it must be Christ-centered. We have no hope beyond death except by analogy with Jesus, who died and rose again.[15]

Third, our hope for life after death must rest firmly on faith in the power of God. If life is life, then death is death and will ever remain so unless and until God intervenes.[16]

Fourth, the bereaved need a theology of death that gives validity to the human experience of suffering.[17] In other words, it must be true to life. We have truly lost someone, and that loss really hurts.

Finally, a theology for the grieving must base all hope for the future on the doctrine of bodily resurrection, i.e., restoration to life of the whole person.[18]

Joseph's last words reflect his hope in God's power. "Take my bones to the Promised Land," he commanded (see Heb. 11:22). No doubt he envisioned the day when, through God's gracious blessing and almighty power, he would be alive again—bodily—and taste that promised blessing for himself. In the end Joseph's hope for life after death rested squarely on faith in the power of the living God. Death is total cessation and will ever remain so unless and until God intervenes—unless God visits! And He will! The glorious truth of Scripture is that: "I know that my Redeemer lives, and He shall stand at last on the earth; and after my skin is destroyed, this I know, that in my flesh I shall see God, whom I shall see for myself, and my eyes shall behold, and not another. How my heart yearns within me!" (Job 19:25-27, NKJV).

"For the Lord Himself will descend from heaven with a shout, with the voice of the archangel, and with the trumpet of God; and the dead in Christ shall rise first" (1 Thess. 4:16).

God Will Surely Visit You!

After a series of defeats from Dunkirk to Singapore, Winston Churchill could finally tell England's House of Commons that "we have a new experience, we have victory." It was November 1942, and Generals Alexander and Montgomery had turned back Rommel's forces at El Alamein, thus winning what Churchill called "The Battle of Egypt." Rommel's army had not just been defeated—it had been thoroughly routed and largely destroyed as a fighting force. Four German divisions and eight Italian divisions had ceased to exist as fighting formations. The Allies had taken 30,000 prisoners along with enormous masses of materials of all kinds. With the larger war in view, Churchill quipped, "This is not the end. It is not even the beginning of the end. But it is, perhaps, the end of the beginning."[19]

As the book of beginnings, Genesis never really ends. The closing words about Joseph do not bring us to the end, or even the beginning of the end. They are, though, certainly the end of the beginning!

Joseph's story ends in Egypt, awaiting the divine visit. "God will surely visit you" Joseph twice says (Gen. 50:24, 25, NKJV). As Brueggemann writes: "That is the Genesis. The visit of God creates possibility for another beginning. By 50:26, we are still at the beginning, still at Genesis awaiting God's newness."[20]

Joseph dies hopeful of a new genesis. "God has sworn his word. God keeps his word. And so there is a waiting."[21]

Joseph spent his whole life living his dreams (Gen. 45:4-11). On the face of it, the dreams appear to end when Joseph is embalmed and placed in a coffin in Egypt. But those dreams were but a part of a larger promise for God's people, and Joseph calls us toward that magnificent picture. He invites us to believe and wait for God's gracious visit in behalf of His promise. You will remember how in the beginning Genesis spoke of God's making everything good (Gen. 1:31), giving man and woman everything they need (Gen. 2:8, 9). He blesses them (Gen. 1:28). But Genesis is the story of people ever seeking the blessing—seeking the blessing their own way, in their own time, in their own strength, and with their own idea of what that blessing really is (Gen. 3:6; 4:3; 16:1-6; 27:1-38). Jacob's haunting cry at Jabbok mirrors the loneliness of every human heart in this book of beginnings: "I will not let you go unless you bless me" (Gen. 32:26). What is the blessing? Where is it? How can I experience it? Genesis ends with the reality that the long-sought blessing of life and peace still comes, and ever will come, only with God, in

His way, in His time, and in His power. And so there is always waiting for the human family, for you and me. Waiting upon God.

It comes down to faith. Hebrews tells us that "by faith Joseph, when he was dying, made mention of the exodus of the sons of Israel, and gave orders concerning his bones" (Heb. 11:22).

When we put on Joseph's colorful tunic and dream of a people as faithful as he, we envision them waiting for God's promised visit. We imagine a people confident in the future, not because of works of righteousness but because of the Righteous One who works in our behalf.

> "We have this hope that burns within our hearts,
> Hope in the coming of the Lord.
> We have this faith that Christ alone imparts,
> Faith in the promise of His Word.
> We believe the time is here, when the nations far and near
> Shall awake, and shout, and sing—Hallelujah! Christ is King!
> We have this hope that burns within our hearts,
> Hope in the coming of the Lord."[22]

---

[1] Always a practical people, the Egyptians assumed that a statue, a painting, or just one's name could serve as an emergency home for the deceased if anything happened to the physical body.

[2] James Hamilton-Paterson and Carol Andrews, *Mummies: Death and Life in Ancient Egypt* (Penguin Books, 1979), p. 66.

[3] *Ibid.*, p. 85. See Janine Bourriau, *Pharaohs and Mortals: Egyptian Art in the Middle Kingdom* (Cambridge: Cambridge University Press, 1988), p. 157.

[4] Hamilton-Paterson and Andrews, p. 66.

[5] *Ibid.*

[6] A. J. Spencer, *Death in Ancient Egypt* (Penguin Books, 1982), p. 144.

[7] *Ibid.*, pp. 145, 146. "The very elevated moral standards revealed by the statements in the address to the gods may have served as an underlying force for righteous conduct in ancient Egypt. It is clear that everyone knew the correct way to act, and even if they might fall short of the righteous path from time to time, the very existence of such knowledge would tend to preserve a tolerant society. The Book of the Dead recognized the fact that people were not faultless and attempted to protect them from the consequences of their sins by the magical spells" (*ibid.*, p. 146).

[8] *Ibid.*, p. 145.

[9] E. H. Peterson, *Leap Over a Wall*, p. 217.

[10] *Ibid.*, pp. 217, 218.

[11] Geoff Walters is minister of Ashford Baptist Church in Kent, England.

[12] Geoff Walters, *Why Do Christians Find It Hard to Grieve?* (Carlisle, Eng.: Paternoster Press, 1997), p. 181.

[13] *Ibid.,* p. 187.

[14] *Ibid.,* p. 185.

[15] *Ibid.,* pp. 185, 186.

[16] *Ibid.,* p. 186.

[17] *Ibid.*

[18] *Ibid.,* pp. 186, 187.

[19] Winston Churchill, "The End of the Beginning," Nov. 10, 1942 (excerpt of speech given by Winston Churchill at the lord mayor's luncheon, Mansion House). See Winston Churchill, *The Second World War* (New York: Time, Inc., 1959), vol. 1, pp. 283, 284.

[20] W. Brueggemann, *Genesis,* p. 379.

[21] *Ibid.*

[22] Wayne Hooper, "We Have This Hope," *The Seventh-day Adventist Hymnal,* No. 214. Used by permission.

The Visitor

From the beginning we have asserted that "the picture of Joseph is an anticipation of what might yet still be, if only God's people would, like Joseph, live in complete obedience and trust in God."[1] As we read his story and reflect on his life, it personally calls every one of us to put on his colorful tunic and dream of being such a man or a woman (a people) as faithful as he. To become "a man for all seasons" or "a woman for all seasons." Not only can Christians today come forth unsullied and unpolluted as he,[2] but God's people are to be to the world what Joseph was to Egypt—a saving influence, a saving presence, a light bearer.[3] Like Joseph, God summons you and me to represent to the world God's character through obedient faithfulness. It is an incredible calling and an awesome privilege and responsibility. God will empower us accordingly. We, too, can conquer life's difficult challenges through Him.

Some have suggested that the story of Joseph looks backward toward Adam.[4] At many points in the story the narrator seems to represent Joseph as the ideal human being. On several occasions Genesis appears to be suggesting that Joseph accomplishes under difficult circumstances what Adam failed to do in a perfect environment. Such scholars see the story of Joseph as "a reflection of what might have been, had Adam remained obedient to God and trusted him for the 'good.'"[5] Surely these evocative parallels pull our minds toward those epochal final moments in earth's history when God will have a people whose faithfulness outstrips any other generation—when the stakes in the great controversy are at their highest.

Is it possible that as this "book of beginnings" *ends* with a picture of this kind of unswerving, relentless faithfulness, that the closing chapters of this world's history will *begin* with the same kind of faithfulness? For sure! Revelation, "the book of endings" tells us so.

But most important, there, between Genesis' troubled beginning and Revelation's glorious ending, is *The Visitor*. The picture of Joseph looks forward to one who was yet to come. The one from the house of Judah "to whom the kingdom belongs" (Gen 49:10).[6] You cannot read the story of Joseph long without seeing Christ, without acquiring a sense of God's way of saving people. Joseph points us to Christ. In fact, Joseph is the most complete type of Christ in the book of Genesis.[7] Some count more than a hundred incidents and details in the Joseph story that, in their opinion, point beyond any question to Christ.[8] While some of these similarities verge on allegory, many are clear, strong parallels. "The integrity of Joseph and his wonderful work in preserving the lives of the whole Egyptian people were a representation of the life of Christ."[9]

Take a moment to consider a few of the parallels: "The life of Joseph illustrates the life of Christ. It was envy that moved the brothers of Joseph to sell him as a slave; they hoped to prevent him from becoming greater than themselves. And when he was carried to Egypt, they flattered themselves that they were to be no more troubled with his dreams, that they had removed all possibility of their fulfillment. But their own course was overruled by God to bring about the very event they designed to hinder. So the Jewish priests and elders were jealous of Christ, fearing that He would attract the attention of the people from them. They put Him to death, to prevent Him from becoming king, but they were thus bringing about this very result. Joseph, through his bondage in Egypt, became a savior to his father's family; yet this fact did not lessen the guilt of his brothers. So the crucifixion of Christ by his enemies made Him the Redeemer of mankind, the Saviour of the fallen race, and Ruler over the whole world; but the crime of His murderers was just as heinous as though God's providential hand had not controlled events for His own glory and the good of man. As Joseph was sold to the heathen by his own brothers, so Christ was sold to His bitterest enemies by one of His disciples. Joseph was falsely accused and thrust into prison because of his virtue; so Christ was despised and rejected because His righteous, self-denying life was a rebuke to sin; and though guilty of no wrong, He was condemned upon the testimony of false witnesses. And Joseph's patience and meekness under injustice and oppression, his ready forgiveness and noble benevolence toward his unnatural brothers, represent the Saviour's uncomplaining endurance of malice and abuse of wicked men, and His forgiveness, not only of His murderers, but of all who have come to Him confessing their sins and seeking pardon."[10]

When we put on Joseph's colorful tunic and dream of a people as faithful as he, we must forever know that it is not a call to human perfection. That in the end, only Christ fulfills the dream. Only He exceeds that image, doing under difficult circumstances what Adam failed to accomplish under perfect conditions (Rom. 5:12-21). Because of Christ's faithfulness, God is able "to preserve many people alive" (Gen. 50:20), including you and me. Departure from Egypt will come, but it is possible only through Him. Conquering life's difficult challenges is His incredible gift as we open our hearts to His gracious work.

Be of faith, then, and dream well, "God will surely visit you" too!

[1] Sailhamer, p. 215.

[2] Ellen G. White, *Medical Ministry*, p. 39.

[3] ———, *Testimonies*, vol. 6, pp. 217, 219.

[4] Sailhamer, p. 215.

[5] *Ibid.*, p. 215.

[6] *Ibid.*

[7] M. R. De Haan, *Portraits of Christ in Genesis* (Grand Rapids: Kregal Publications, 1995), pp. 163, 178.

[8] *Ibid.*, p. 163.

[9] Ellen G. White, *Christ's Object Lessons* (Washington, D.C.: Review and Herald Pub. Assn., 1941), p. 286.

[10] White, *Patriarchs and Prophets*, pp. 239, 240.